To Eddie

Best Wishes

TH

ANOTHER
100 OF THE BEST

ANOTHER
100 OF THE BEST

DARLINGTON'S GREATEST EVER PLAYERS

PAUL HODGSON

pitch

First published by Pitch Publishing, 2025

pitch

Pitch Publishing
9 Donnington Park,
85 Birdham Road,
Chichester, West Sussex,
PO20 7AJ
www.pitchpublishing.co.uk
info@pitchpublishing.co.uk

A CIP catalogue record is available for this book
from the British Library.

ISBN 978 1 80150 929 9

MIX
Paper | Supporting
responsible forestry
FSC
www.fsc.org   FSC™ C016779

Printed and bound on FSC® certified paper in line with
our continuing commitment to ethical business practices,
sustainability and the environment.

Typesetting and origination by Pitch Publishing
Printed and bound in India by Replika Press Pvt. Ltd.

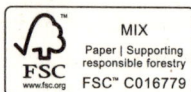

Contents

For my wife, Jennifer,
who is my soulmate and
best friend.

Acknowledgements

THANKS TO Jane Camillin at Pitch Publishing for all her support and, as per usual, her patience – plus the editing team at Pitch. Thanks to my wife Jennifer for her never-ending patience, and my PA Chris for his constant practical help. I'd like to say a massive thank you to all the Darlo fans for their support along the way, especially Ian Carter, Stephen Lowson and John Gray – all of whom feature in this book. In addition, I'd like to thank the following ex-Darlington players for giving me their time and details about what they did after they finished playing: Mark Forster, Kevan Smith, David Speedie, Alan Walsh, Roger Wicks, Peter Kirkham, Simon Shaw, Craig Liddle, Robbie Painter, Gary Twynham, Glenn Naylor, Michael Oliver, Mark Sheeran, Michael Smith, Graeme Armstrong, Nathan Cartman, Gary Brown, Jack Winstanley, Leo Pontone and Ciaran Dixon, as well as ex-Chelsea, Middlesbrough, Leyton Orient, Scunthorpe United, Lincoln City and Gainsborough Trinity midfielder, but more importantly, former Darlington player and manager Paul Ward, who kindly wrote the foreword for this book. I'm extremely grateful to him for doing this for me.

Finally, I'd like to express my sincere thanks to freelance writer Simon Weatherill for allowing me to use some of his material. Last but by no means least, I'm extremely grateful to current Darlington FC CEO David Johnston for the help and support he has given me with this, and indeed the many other projects I have undertaken since we met.

Foreword by Paul Ward

I WOULD like to begin by saying what an honour it is to be asked by Paul to write the foreword to his latest book. He is a real inspiration and someone I am very proud to call a friend.

It was September 1985 when, along with Alan Roberts, I travelled the well-trodden path from Middlesbrough to Darlington. The club was full of familiar faces. The management team were obviously well known to us and the dressing room was full of former team-mates. I immediately sensed an overwhelming feeling of warmth and welcome in my new home I grew to love, called Feethams.

That welcoming feeling wasn't so forthcoming from sections of the crowd after a difficult start to our time at Darlington. However, one man stood out from the crowd (the irony of which won't be lost on him). My very first encounter with Paul ('Flipper') Hodgson was after another negative result, in a tightly fought contest versus Notts County. I was introduced to him in the cricket club, where we had our post-match pint in those days. Rather than being met with a belligerent attitude, I was immediately struck by his pragmatic approach to supporting his beloved Darlington. What became clear after that first encounter was not only his obvious love of the club, but here was a man who had a real knowledge of the game. The conversation was about the tactics and where he thought we'd got it right in some areas and wrong in others. Paul was totally respectful with his opinion and made a lot of sense. It wasn't the last time I was to have the benefit of his opinion on formation or tactics. Paul was a constant fixture, home or away; no matter the distance or logistics, he found a way to get there, and this was very much appreciated by us all. It wasn't uncommon for him to grab a ride home on the team coach either.

During my second season I was given the honour of becoming player-manager, with the club in a precarious position at the foot of the table. We were playing Mansfield Town away at Field Mill, and as the coach pulled up there was a noticeable billow of smoke which looked to be coming from the stadium. As we got off the coach, a few of the supporters were there to greet us, and informed us the game wasn't in doubt as the fire was in an adjacent building, far enough away, so as not to affect the fixture. I noticed Paul as one of those supporters, said 'hello' and he immediately summoned me over. Now picture the scene that followed, as the recently appointed player-manager is pushing Paul up the hill towards the entrance to the ground in his wheelchair. The conversation turned immediately to the game, touching on selection, formation and tactics. Once again, I have to say how impressed I was with his knowledge and thoughts on how things should go, but the one thing that has always stood out for me is his unwavering positive outlook and optimism. I personally think this is Paul's attitude to life, and no challenge or obstacle is too great.

To this day I have remained in touch with Paul, some 35 years after leaving Darlington. We often chat on the phone, and believe me it's never a quick chat. Over the years Paul has organised a few charity games, with former players turning up to support him, just as he supported us. I'm sure whatever he plans in the future, that same support will be there from us all.

Congratulations on your life's work so far Paul and I wish you continued success with your future projects.

Forever a friend, Wardy

Paul Ward, Darlington 1985–1988

Introduction

GREATEST PLAYERS in my opinion aren't always superstars who play in the Champions League and Premier League title deciders, which, as a lifelong Darlington fan, is just as well as I would have been struggling to fill this book! But as any Quakers fan will tell you, there have been plenty of unforgettable players who have represented the club over the 51 years that I've supported them.

Our memories as Quakers fans are filled with just as much drama and rollercoaster moments – our club more than most – and they are what I've tried to capture in this book. While most of the players you would expect to find in a collection such as this are indeed here, there are a few others who might evoke some raised eyebrows and a couple that might even raise the question, 'Why?' Well, there's a reason behind each one and while some may be more obvious than others, I hope you enjoy reading about one or two gems who might have otherwise been forgotten and confined to a stat in a history book. I reckon the next few years will probably yield another 20 or so new lads who could live happily in this book. However, here are 100 who should certainly stick in my memory banks for one reason or another. Enjoy the book and many thanks for buying it.

1

Goalkeepers

Phil Owers – Career Details

Phil Owers began his football career with Shildon, making his senior debut as a 15-year-old, before signing for the then Fourth Division strugglers Darlington. While still an A-level student, Owers made his first appearance in the Football League, on 6 January 1973; the Quakers conceded seven goals to Southport, though no more than one was attributable to the goalkeeper. The local *Northern Echo* newspaper reported, 'He was in no way to blame for the disgraceful shambles, but looked close to tears as he was applauded down the tunnel.' A few weeks later, Owers was interviewed by David Frost for an edition of *The Frost Programme*, focusing on Darlington Football Club as an illustration of the unglamorous side of football, described 40 years later by the *Northern Echo* as 'an insight into a town's heart-aching relationship with its football club and a reminder of the ridiculous resilience of optimism'. Described by Frost as '17 and nursing a dream', Owers said he 'wanted to get Darlington out of trouble and would like to play at Wembley for a big club'.

Over the next two and a half seasons, he made 45 league appearances before signing for the then Third Division club Gillingham on a free transfer. He played only twice for the Gills and returned to Darlington after only one season. After 69 more matches in the Fourth Division over a four-year period, Owers moved back into non-league football with Crook Town and then with Bishop Auckland. He was a member of the Bishops' Northern League title-winning team in 1984/85. After a spell with Brandon United, he played four matches on a non-contract basis for Fourth Division Hartlepool United in August 1987, before a further spell at Bishop Auckland and also a stint with Spennymoor United.

By 1993 he was back at Shildon as a player and left as assistant manager in 1999. Back again by April 2003, he was reported to have played for the club in four different decades. Later that year he was on the bench as Shildon reached the first round proper of the 2003/04 FA Cup, when they lost 7-2 to then Second Division club Notts County.

Owers continued to play into his 50s. He won the Durham Alliance title with Shildon Railway in 2004/05, and appeared in the Northern League while manager of West Auckland Town in April 2008 at the age of 52.

My Memorable Match Involving Phil Owers
Darlington v Southport – 1972/73

The first Darlington game I ever saw was at a fog-shrouded Feethams on 6 January 1973 when I was only seven years old. Our visitors that day were Southport, who at the time were promotion contenders, while the Quakers were firmly rooted to the bottom of the Fourth Division.

Our home fixture against Workington on Boxing Day had already been postponed because a mixture of injuries and a flu epidemic had reduced Darlington to just eight fit players, and because of the foggy conditions the Southport game was only given the go-ahead by the referee an hour before kick-off.

Allan Jones, who had been sent on a three-week 'holiday' by the chairman, George Tait, had officially parted company with the club on 21 December. He became the fourth Darlington manager to lose his job in only 15 months. His replacement was Ralph Brand.

The previous game, on 23 December 1972, was away to Bradford City where we were hammered 7-0. Apparently, after the match at Valley Parade the newly installed manager assured the press that the result had been a 'one-off' and that they would never be beaten like that again. Clearly, he didn't believe, and neither did I, that lightning would strike twice.

Ironically, Brand had an impressive pedigree as a player and knew all about scoring goals. Born in Edinburgh, he had played for Rangers, notching an impressive 206 goals in 317 games for the Ibrox club. He even ranks third among their postwar strikers, just behind Ally McCoist and Derek Johnstone.

However, the omens certainly didn't look good for the visit of Southport. On the day of the match, with only an hour to go before kick-off, Phil Owers, a 17-year-old rookie goalkeeper was called upon to make his first-team debut in place of regular shot-stopper Ernie Adams, who couldn't play due to injury.

The match was certainly a one-sided affair. By half-time the Quakers were 4-0 down and they went on to lose 7-0, which is their heaviest ever home league defeat to date. To cap it all I'd pestered my mother for weeks on end to take me to a Darlington game! My abiding memory was, 'Why have I come down here in the middle of winter in the freezing cold?'

Throughout the match and as the avalanche of goals came thick and fast, much to the anger of some of the crowd, Brand remained in his seat in the directors' box instead of coming down to the touchline to encourage his players. His semi-detached attitude to management was exemplified by the fact that he actually lived in Edinburgh where he was in business and only commuted to Darlington each Wednesday where he remained until the following Saturday evening.

At the final whistle the fans gave Phil Owers a standing ovation. After all, he wasn't to blame for the rout. Had it not been for his bravery and agility, we might have eclipsed our heaviest ever league defeat when we lost 10-0 away to Doncaster on 25 January 1964.

Thinking about it, I bet that hasn't happened very often in professional football – two consecutive 7-0 defeats with two different goalkeepers.

* * *

Martin Burleigh – Career Details

Martin Burleigh was born in Willington, County Durham. He played football for his hometown club, before joining Newcastle United as a 17-year-old, signing amateur forms in October 1968. He replaced the injured Dave Clarke in a strong Newcastle team for Barrie Thomas's testimonial match in November and turned professional in the December of that year. Burleigh was also a member of the Newcastle United youth team that won the 1969 Rotterdam International Youth Tournament, defeating Arsenal's youngsters in the final.

He made his first-team debut on 26 December 1970, in a 3-0 defeat away to Leeds United in the First Division. Martin had to wait over a year before making another senior appearance. His home debut came on 8 January 1972 in a 4-2 league victory over Coventry City.

An injury to undisputed first-choice goalkeeper Willie 'Iam' McFaul in February 1973 allowed Martin a run of games in the first team, which ended when his left index finger was broken by a kick from Mick Channon during a 1-1 draw away to Southampton and he was ruled out for the rest of the season. A dispute with manager Joe Harvey stemming from his return to pre-season training seriously overweight caused him to walk out of the club. He returned, but played only twice more, the last of his 15 first-team appearances for Newcastle coming on 11 May 1974 against Tottenham Hotspur at St James' Park. When he again reported overweight for the 1974/75 season, the club threatened to cancel his contract, at which point he resigned and considered joining the RAF.

The club retained Burleigh's Football League registration and loaned him to Darlington in October 1974, and made the transfer permanent in December for a fee reported as £3,000 plus 50 per cent of the profit on any future sale. He spent that season as Darlington's first-choice goalkeeper, and then moved on to Carlisle United, newly relegated to the Second Division, in June 1975. Although a transfer request was accepted in

November that same year, Burleigh remained with Carlisle until 1977. He then returned to Darlington for a further two-year spell; in the first he was the club's player of the season. He finished his professional career with three seasons at then Fourth Division Hartlepool United, for whom he made 96 appearances in all competitions before moving into non-league football in 1982 with Bishop Auckland and then playing for Spennymoor United and Langley Park.

After his professional football career ended, Burleigh worked as a painter and decorator based in Ferryhill, County Durham. He died on 27 September 2021 at the age of 70.

My Memorable Match Involving Martin Burleigh

Everton v Darlington – League Cup third round 1978/79

Unfortunately, I couldn't go to this match because I was at boarding school at the time. But I feel that I must include it because it was one of Martin's best games for Darlington. I can remember as if it were yesterday, being glued to the radio in my bedroom at boarding school listening to the game. Here's what I recall. It goes without saying that I have checked the facts using an old match report, (kindly supplied by Simon Weatherill) given that I was a child at the time the match was played.

As I listened to the radio, I quickly realised that Darlington had packed their defence and in the early stages had easily snuffed out the home team's forwards, Bob Latchford and Mick Walsh. However, they missed a golden opportunity in the 16th minute when Jimmy Cochrane's free kick from the left was headed down by centre-half Derek Craig to striker Jimmy Seal, who miscued his shot from six yards and the ball ended up in the arms of an extremely grateful Everton goalkeeper George Wood; the chance was gone. The home side came more into the game and Martin Burleigh made a brilliant save from Andy King in the 37th minute. The visitors continued to cause their First Division opponents problems and just before the interval, Wood grabbed the ball off John Stone's head, following an excellent free kick from Quakers winger Dennis Wann.

Burleigh was the first keeper to make a save of any worth in the second half when in the 54th minute he dived full length to keep out a rasping 20-yard drive from Everton midfielder Geoff Nulty. Shortly after that, the home side took the lead. Future Darlington manager Colin Todd crossed, King flicked it on and midfielder Martin Dobson slotted the ball home. Not long after his goal, Dobson thought that he'd doubled the lead when he put the ball in the net following a weak back-pass from defender Clive Nattress, but it was chalked off for offside. Just prior to that, Stone had blasted a free kick wide for Darlington after Lloyd Maitland had been brought down by Nulty 30 yards out. The Quakers continued to press and in the 60th minute Wann put another 30-yard free kick inches wide with Wood well beaten. Later in the game, Wood was in trouble again when he handled outside the box. Unfortunately for the visitors, captain Barry Lyons blasted the free kick just wide of the post with Wood again struggling. In the final ten minutes, Peter Madden's men laid siege to the Everton goal, but the home team held out to ensure their somewhat lucky passage into the fourth round.

As I switched my radio off, I can remember thinking that I was proud of my team and wished I'd been there to witness such a brilliant Darlington performance.

* * *

Pat Cuff – Career Details

Pat Cuff was born in Middlesbrough and was an English schoolboy international.

He began his football career as an apprentice with his hometown club in 1968. He made his debut in the Football League while on loan at Grimsby Town in the 1971/72 season, but had to wait until April 1974 for his Middlesbrough debut, by which time the club had already won the Second Division title. He continued as backup to regular goalkeeper and future Darlington manager Jim Platt, until a dispute between Platt and manager Jack Charlton in late 1976 gave Cuff a run in the side.

Pat finished his Middlesbrough career with 31 league appearances, and moved to Millwall in the 1978 close-season on a free transfer. He spent two seasons at The Den and in 1978/79 he was ever-present with 46 appearances in league and cups as the club were relegated to the Third Division but then lost his place to new signing John Jackson and never played for the first team again.

After three years in the then Fourth Division with Darlington, which took his total league appearances to 185, Cuff retired, and later became a bookmaker.

Interestingly, his son Phil played rugby union for West Hartlepool.

My Memorable Match Involving Pat Cuff
Darlington v Doncaster Rovers – 1980/81

I went to this game with my mother. I have to say, the pair of us saw a brilliant second half from the Quakers.

The hosts made a strong start but they found the Rovers defence to be in a determined mood, with goalkeeper Willie Boyd in inspired form. Darlington dominated the first half with some slick, attacking play but couldn't find the breakthrough. Boyd made superb saves from John Stalker and Alan Walsh and several other chances went begging.

It took Darlington only four minutes of the second half to grab the lead. Rovers skipper Hugh Dowd played a wayward back-pass towards his keeper and striker Stalker nipped in and steered the ball home. Ten minutes later Harry Charlton sent Walsh away down the right and he finished off a 50-yard run with a trademark powerful cross-come-shot just inside the far post. It was truly a brilliant goal! In a rare attack, Stewart Mell went close for the visitors, before Dave Hawker scored Darlington's third after 72 minutes, Stalker finding him with a neat pass across the edge of the box and the midfielder firing a low, hard drive into the corner of the net. David Speedie created the fourth when he broke through the middle and unselfishly pushed the ball into Charlton's path and he picked his spot from 12 yards out. The scoring was completed on 84 minutes when a Stalker cross was handled by Pat Lally and Hamilton drove home the penalty. Five unanswered second-half goals had completely destroyed Billy Bremner's team.

As my mother pushed me home, I can remember saying to her that I could have played in goal in my wheelchair as Pat Cuff was a bystander for almost the whole game. That's why this match always reminds me of Cuffy – because of that throwaway comment.

* * *

Fred Barber – Career Details

Born in Ferryhill, County Durham, Fred Barber began his career at Darlington in 1979, where he served his apprenticeship. He made 135 Football League appearances for the club before a £50,000 move to First Division champions Everton in April 1986.

He was signed as understudy to Neville Southall but after six months and no first-team appearances for Everton, Barber was sold to Walsall for £100,000. In his second season with the club, Walsall were promoted to the then Second Division, but then suffered successive relegations. Fred was loaned out to Peterborough United in 1989/90, where he made six appearances. He was again loaned out in 1990/91 to Chester City on two occasions, in October 1990 and March 1991, accumulating eight appearances, and to Blackpool in November 1990 where he played twice. He also made appearances for Walsall during the same campaign, but moved to Peterborough on a permanent basis in the summer of 1991 for a £25,000 fee. Fred made a total of 153 appearances for Walsall between 1986 and 1991.

He made his second debut for Peterborough on 17 August 1991, keeping a clean sheet against Preston North End in a 1-0 victory. He helped the club to promotion to the Second Division with a 1992 play-off final victory over Stockport County, but they struggled in the second tier and Barber found himself out on loan once again, at Chesterfield in February 1993, but he didn't make an appearance for the Spireites. He was then sent on loan to Colchester United, making his debut on 20 March 1993 in a 2-0 victory for the U's at Brunton Park against Carlisle United. He made ten appearances for Colchester before returning to Peterborough. In the following season, despite Peterborough finishing bottom of the Second Division, Luton Town made a £25,000 offer for Barber, and he transferred in August 1994, ending his stay with 63 appearances in three years.

Just four months later, Barber found himself back at London Road with Peterborough. Having made no first-team appearances for Luton, he was sent on loan and played five league games. After this stint, he played one league game first at Ipswich Town in November 1995, and one league game in a return to Blackpool in December 1995. The much-travelled keeper finished his Football League career by joining Birmingham City in 1996, again making just a single appearance. The last club he actively played for was Kidderminster Harriers, where he made 21 Conference appearances before stepping into coaching with Bolton Wanderers, West Bromwich Albion, Northern Ireland, Bury, York City, Oman, Jamaica, Sunderland, Stoke City, Blackpool, Burnley, Bradford City, Stockport County, Rochdale and Crewe Alexandra.

My Memorable Match Involving Fred Barber
Darlington v Stockport County – 1982/83

My mother dropped me off at Feethams for this match and I witnessed a stuttering start from Darlington, who despite their recent improvement in form had still only won one home game in the previous four months. Their nervousness showed as the visitors enjoyed the best of the opening half. County took the lead in the 38th minute with a straightforward corner routine. Dean Emerson's flag kick was met by Tommy Sword who scored with an unstoppable header. They could have increased their lead but Fred Barber, who was making his league debut following an injury to regular number one Pat Cuff, produced two brilliant saves to keep out Nigel Smith and Mike Power. Stockport went into the break with a comfortable 1-0 lead, with the Quakers seemingly sliding towards yet another home defeat.

Barber continued his man-of-the-match performance by saving twice more from Power at the start of the second half, before providing an assist for Alan Walsh's equaliser in the 65th minute. He launched a hefty kick deep into Stockport territory that found Walsh breaking through a gap in the centre of County's defence. He rounded visiting keeper Brian Lloyd and slotted into the net from an acute angle. Peter Cartwright, signed on loan from Newcastle United prior to the match, was not to be outdone by his fellow debutant, and then took centre stage by creating the opening for Darlington's second goal in the 75th minute. He ploughed through three tackles in a determined run in central midfield and played a pass out wide to Walsh, who made progress down the left and crossed to the far post, where the ball was met by the onrushing Dave McLean, who headed home. The victory was completed in the last minute when Tony McFadden outpaced three defenders before drawing Lloyd and sliding the ball wide of the advancing keeper. Three goals in the last 25 minutes had turned what looked like being Darlington's eighth home defeat of the season into an important victory that moved them up another two places in the table. Fred Barber continued his great form and kept his place in goal for the remainder of the season. I had seen him develop for three years in the reserve and youth teams, so it came as no surprise to me when he grabbed his first-team opportunity with both hands, so to speak.

* * *

Mike Astbury – Career Details

Mike Astbury became York City's youngest ever goalkeeper when, as a 16-year-old, he played in City's 1-1 draw at Bournemouth in the 1980/81 season. He had spells in and out of the side over the next few years, with one of the highlights being when York surprisingly knocked Arsenal out of the 1984/85 FA

Cup, where some brave goalkeeping from Astbury kept City in the game before their late winner.

He moved to Peterborough United on loan in January 1986, two months before signing permanently for Darlington. Astbury moved on again in July 1987 to Chester City. Injured shortly after arriving, Mike had to wait until December 1987 for his first-team debut. He played in five successive games during the month but was never picked again as Billy Stewart became the regular goalkeeper for the club.

Astbury was released at the end of that season and joined Chesterfield, where just eight league appearances were made in a relegation season from the Third Division. That marked the end of Astbury's professional career as he joined non-league side Gainsborough Trinity.

Mike later emigrated to play in the USA.

My Memorable Match Involving Mike Astbury
Darlington v York City – 1986/87

Darlington's first match of the 1986/87 season was away at York City. I went there on the train with my friend Ian Carter, and two other associates, Malcolm and Clare. Stephen Lowson, who by now had moved to London, travelled up from there and met us at York station for a game in which David Currie, signed from Middlesbrough in the close-season, and former Grimsby player Mark Hine were making their debuts.

Derek Hood scored first for the Minstermen from the penalty spot in the 17th minute after Darlington central defender Phil Lloyd was adjudged to have handled the ball. However, when Tony Canham scored their second goal on the stroke of half-time he appeared to be yards offside, but the linesman didn't raised his flag even after I shouted at him, so I turned my attention to Viv Busby, the York coach, who by that time was jumping up and down celebrating (you'd think his team had already won the league judging by way he went on) and said he must be blind to think that the goal was onside. But he was adamant that it was and simply ignored my protests.

Incidentally, after the press interviewed Denis Smith, the York manager, he later admitted that it *was* offside, after all!

Tony Ford added a third for York in the 55th minute before David Currie scored a consolation goal 11 minutes from time. However, Darlington were well beaten on the day.

Mike Astbury excelled in goal for Darlington against his former club. If it wasn't for him, the Quakers would have lost by a far greater margin.

* * *

Mike Pollitt – Career Details

Born in Farnworth, Lancashire, Mike Pollitt began his career at Manchester United, turning professional in the summer of 1990 following a two year apprenticeship. On 5 October 1990, Pollitt joined Oldham Athletic on a month's loan as backup for Jon Hallworth but did not make a senior appearance during his time at Boundary Park. In January 1991 he joined then Conference side Macclesfield Town, also on loan, debuting in the 1-1 away draw with Boston United on 5 January 1991. After a further appearance in a 2-0 FA Trophy defeat at home to Gretna the following week, he returned to Old Trafford and was released by Alex Ferguson at the end of that season.

The stopper joined Bury ahead of the 1991/92 campaign but was forced to play a supporting role to regular custodian Gary Kelly. On 26 March 1992 he joined Lincoln City on loan for the remainder of the season as cover for Ian Bowling following the departure of Matt Dickins to Blackburn Rovers but was not called upon to make an appearance.

He began the 1992/93 season on loan to Conference side Altrincham, debuting in the 1-0 home defeat to Gateshead on 25 August 1992. He played in the next three league games before heading back to Gigg Lane.

On 24 September 1992, Mike rejoined Lincoln on a month's loan to cover for Bowling who had fractured his foot in a 3-1 League Cup defeat away to Crystal Palace two days previously. He made his Football League debut in the 1-0 home defeat to Shrewsbury Town on 26 September and made five league appearances for the club, one of which came against his parent club Bury, before relinquishing his place to the returning Bowling. Mike, however, remained on loan at Sincil Bank and at the end of the second month Lincoln officially took over the remainder of Pollitt's Bury contract.

Following a brief sojourn to appear a further time for Altrincham in the 2-0 home victory over Welling United on 19 December 1992, he managed to displace Bowling from the Lincoln side over the Christmas fixtures and a series of impressive displays saw him rewarded with a new two-year contract in March 1993. He began 1993/94 as the Imps' first-choice goalkeeper before briefly losing his place to John Burridge, who later also replaced him at Darlington, over the Christmas and New Year fixtures and indeed permanently following the signing of Andy Leaning in March 1994. In the summer, one of the first acts of newly appointed Lincoln manager Sam Ellis was to transfer list Pollitt and Dave Ridings, and Pollitt soon agreed a move to Darlington.

In November 1995, his one-time Lincoln manager Steve Thompson, acting as team manager with Colin Murphy as general manager, paid £75,000 to secure Pollitt's services for Notts County. In his time at Meadow Lane, Pollitt failed to dislodge regular custodian Darren Ward and had to wait until 22 February 1997 before making his County debut in a 2-0 away defeat to former club Bury. Seeking regular first-team football, he was sent out on loan to four clubs during the 1997/98 season.

Mike had two spells at Rotherham United, from 1998 to 2000 and 2001 to 2005. Between these periods was a season at Chesterfield. Pollitt was very highly regarded at the South Yorkshire club and while at Rotherham he registered the highest number of clean sheets, 77, in their history. After serving the Millers for six years, Pollitt is still regarded as a Rotherham legend and one of the best keepers in their history, if not *the* best.

Wigan Athletic acquired his services from Rotherham in June 2005. Prior to Rotherham, Pollitt had also played for

Oldham Athletic and Sunderland but his move to Wigan, initially as cover for John Filan, following advice from Paul Barlow, gave him the chance to play Premier League football. His outstanding performances earned him a regular first-team place and in February 2006 he helped his club to a spot in the 2006 League Cup Final. In the semi-final he saved a penalty from Arsenal's José Antonio Reyes to help the Latics triumph. In the final itself a hamstring injury in the opening minutes meant that he had to be substituted after quarter of an hour, and he was replaced by Filan.

In November 2006, Mike joined Ipswich Town on loan for a month. However, he was recalled by Wigan after only one game because of injury worries within their squad. He was then loaned to Burnley for a month in January 2007. He played four matches for them and was recalled with one match left on his loan deal after Wigan's Chris Kirkland picked up an injury. He agreed a new one year contract with Wigan in May 2009 and subsequently extended his deal by another year in May 2010. A further year was added in July 2011, which ensured that he remained at the club after his 40th birthday. His stay was extended to an eighth season when he agreed a further one-year contract extension in June 2012, where he was second choice to Ali Al-Habsi for the 2010/11 and 2011/12 seasons. He made his first competitive start for Wigan in more than two years against Bournemouth in the FA Cup on 5 January 2013 and he also started the replay but was substituted at half-time due to an injury. At the end of the season he had his contract extended by another year. On 27 August 2013, he joined fellow Championship side Barnsley on a month's loan.

Mike called time on his long playing career at the end of the 2013/14 season. He'd played a total of 52 games for Wigan in nine years.

After finishing playing, Mike continued to coach at Wigan, before moving on to Rotherham, Bolton Wanderers and Preston North End.

My Memorable Match Involving Mike Pollitt

Hartlepool United v Darlington, FA Cup first round – 1995/96

I went to the above match with Ian in his car and I can remember being super excited at facing our local rivals, especially in the FA Cup.

The pair of us saw the home side make the better start, and they had the Quakers on the back foot early on. Ex-Darlington player Mick Tait could and indeed should have opened the scoring in the 8th minute when Mike Pollitt failed to collect a cross, and Tait chipped wide of the empty net from 20 yards out. A minute later Stephen Halliday burst between two defenders but fired his shot straight at Pollitt.

Pools got the lead that their early play deserved in the 13th minute. A neat, flicked ball forward by Halliday found Scott Sloan on the edge of the box and he superbly volleyed first time into the top-right corner. They very nearly increased their lead two minutes later when a good run by Halliday finished with a thumping drive just wide of the post. Darlington began to find their feet on the difficult surface and equalised on 25 minutes. Steve Gaughan beat the offside trap and raced clear down the right before squaring the ball to the far post where Phil Brumwell slid in and fired home. The Quakers were well on top now and took the lead with an almost carbon copy goal in the 37th minute. This time it was Paul Olsson who made progress down the right, hurdling a challenge from full-back Ian McGuckin and crossing to the far post where Gaughan forced the ball home with a close range header, to make the half-time score 2-1 to my beloved Darlington.

During the interval, Ian and I stayed in the disabled area because the queues for food and drink were far too long, so we did without. This gave us plenty of chance to chat about the second half. We were both confident that the Quakers would be in the hat for the second round.

Darlington began the second half as they had finished the first – in total control. They increased their lead in the 59th minute when Gaughan put Robbie Painter through on goal, but Pools keeper Brian Horne made a good save at the striker's feet. However, he couldn't hold the ball, which ran loose back to Gaughan, who squared the rebound to Gary Bannister and he lashed his shot into the roof of the net from near the penalty spot. They kept pressing forward and made the game safe five minutes later when Matty Appleby played a great ball down the right to Painter, who this time made no mistake, cutting inside and drilling home from the corner of the box.

With being 4-1 in front the visitors eased off and allowed Pools back into the game. Halliday scored a well-taken goal on 75 minutes, although he looked suspiciously offside when he cut in from the left and fired home off the body of Pollitt. In a spirited finish Pools went close again when Pollitt saved superbly from Sloan and in the ensuing goalmouth scramble Simon Shaw seemed to handle the ball but somehow escaped conceding a penalty. The Quakers had started slowly and finished sloppily but in between they had been devastating and fully deserved their 4-2 win.

This match proved to be Mike Pollitt's last in a Darlington shirt. Immediately after the game he was sold to Notts County, which led shortly afterwards to the resignation of manager David Hodgson.

This is part of the reason I think of Mike when I look back to that match. I was also disappointed to learn that David Hodgson had left. Ian and I didn't know anything about this as we celebrated our victory in Darlington town centre, following our train journey home.

* * *

Mark Prudhoe – Career Details

Mark Prudhoe was born in Washington, County Durham, and began his career with Sunderland. After a loan spell with Hartlepool United in 1983, Mark had further short spells with Birmingham City, Walsall, Doncaster Rovers, Sheffield Wednesday, Grimsby Town, a second loan to Hartlepool,

Bristol City and Carlisle United. He then joined Darlington in 1989, where he picked up winners' medals for the Conference and the Fourth Division, as well as the Conference Shield.

This success earned him a move to Stoke City where he played 38 times in 1993/94, 48 times in 1995/96 and 15 in 1996/97. While at Stoke, Mark spent time out on loan at Peterborough United, Liverpool and York City. He then went on to play for Bradford City, a second spell at Darlington, Southend United, a second spell at Bradford and he finally ended his career at Macclesfield Town in 2003/04.

After he finished playing, Mark had a coaching spell at Hull City from 2003 to 2011, before returning to Sunderland, where he remains at the time of writing.

My Memorable Match Involving Mark Prudhoe
Northwich Victoria v Darlington – 1989/90

I chose this match for Mark Prudhoe for a reason that will become apparent later.

As a matter of interest, Northwich Victoria were one of four former league sides in the Conference that season, if you included Darlington – the other two being Merthyr Tydfil and Barrow. In fact, they were founder members of the Second Division in 1892, but they only lasted two seasons before they dropped out of the league in 1894, never to return.

This was Darlington's third meeting with Northwich that season as they had already comprehensively beaten them 4-0 in the league and 6-2 in the first round of the FA Cup.

After I'd left work, my father dropped me off at Catterick Bridge, close to where Ian works. Ian then drove me the rest of the way and we parked in a side street near the ground, arriving just in time for the evening kick-off.

Unlike the previous two matches, this game was a brutal affair. The home side resorted to the most cynical tactics, which amounted to literally kicking our players off the pitch. There was even a rumour going around that the chairman of one of our promotion rivals had offered the Northwich players £1,000 per man to stop us from winning the game, though I should add that this was never actually substantiated.

In the 14th minute, our midfielder Neil Robinson had to leave the field after he was on the receiving end of a two-footed tackle, and his ankle ligament damage was so serious that he was unable to play professional football again. On top of that, in the 35th minute, Kevan Smith sustained a head wound that required several stitches. As he lay on the pitch receiving treatment from our physio, an old woman in the Northwich end shouted, 'I hope he's swallowed his tongue and he dies.' After ten minutes of treatment Kevan returned to the fray with his head swathed in bandages. He required further attention later as his stitches burst open during the game and the wound had to be re-stitched.

In the 55th minute the hosts scored. Then, two minutes later, Mark Prudhoe and John Stringer both went for a 50-50 ball. Prudhoe came out worst, and received a nasty gash to his thigh from the opposing player's raking studs and had to be stretchered off. He was then taken to the local hospital where he was kept in overnight for observation. The tackle that caused this appalling injury was only punished with a booking, and yet it kept Prudhoe out of the side for more than five weeks. After this particular incident, Brian Little and his opposing number, Cliff Roberts, became embroiled in a heated argument, which one of the linesmen managed to bring under control and the end result was that our forward, John Borthwick, went into goal. It was hardly a surprise that we lost this bruising encounter 1-0.

I'll never forget the injury Mark sustained in that match; it was a terrible 'tackle' by John Stringer that could have ended Pruds's career. That's why I chose this match as my memory match for him.

* * *

Andy Collett – Career Details
Andy Collett was born in Stockton-on-Tees. He began his career at Middlesbrough, for whom he made his first-team debut.

He then moved south to Bristol Rovers where he remained for five years before joining Darlington. Andy also stayed with the Quakers for five years, before his career was cut short because of a shoulder injury. However, he played a vital role in helping Darlington reach the 2000 Third Division play-off final, where they lost to Peterborough United at Wembley.

After he finished playing, Andy became Darlington's goalkeeping coach in 2004. On 26 May 2009 he was appointed to the same position at Oldham Athletic. He was reunited with Dave Penney and Martin Gray, who were also among the coaching staff at Darlington. He stayed there until he joined League One club Hartlepool United, again as goalkeeping coach on 15 December 2011. He left in June 2013 when his contract was not renewed upon the club's relegation. Andy soon took up a similar position at League Two club York City before he left in May 2015, but returned in 2017, as well as running a successful coaching academy in Teesside. It was announced that he had left York on 4 April 2022.

My Memorable Match Involving Andy Collett
Darlington v Macclesfield Town – 1999/2000

Ian once again accompanied me for this first home league game of the 1999/2000 season. The pair of us saw a determined and well organised Macclesfield team cancel out most of what Darlington were trying to create. A long ball forward by Brian Atkinson in the ninth minute was met by Marco Gabbiadini at full stretch but the striker could only poke his shot over the bar. Then Lee Nogan almost scored his first goal for the club with a low right-footed shot but he was denied by Macclesfield goalkeeper Ryan Price, diving full length to save. These were virtually the only chances of the first half as the visitors took a vice-like grip on the game. They got men behind the ball, stopped Darlington wing-backs Craig Liddle and Paul Heckingbottom from getting forward and tightly marked Gabbiadini, who barely featured in the game following his early chance.

The second half very nearly began in spectacular fashion. Only 30 seconds after the restart, Liddle played in a deep cross which was flicked on by Heckingbottom and headed towards goal by Gabbiadini but was brilliantly saved by Price. The game then quickly reverted to the pattern of the first half with the visitors' midfield in control of things and their forwards looking increasingly dangerous on the break. However, it all changed completely in the 64th minute with a double substitution and a reshuffle by manager David Hodgson. Off came Adam Reed and Michael Oliver, to be replaced by Martin Carruthers and Neil Heaney, making his Quakers debut. The changes very nearly backfired two minutes later as the home side were reorganising, and Macclesfield created their best chance of the game, but Andy Collett pulled off a superb save to deny Kieron Durkan. Then Chris Priest went close for the visitors when he fired over the bar when well placed, but by this time the influence of Heaney was starting to show. His pace and control gave the hosts a new dimension and his passing and switching of play began to cause the Silkmen's defence all sorts of problems as Darlington began to find space in their opponents' half.

The deadlock was finally broken on 83 minutes. Gabbiadini sent Nogan away down the left and then made his way into the box and crossed to the far post where the waiting Carruthers headed the ball down for Marco to slot it into the bottom corner. Within a minute Darlington were two up as Gabbiadini, Nogan and Martin Gray combined well to release Heaney down the left and he crossed perfectly for Marco to fire in his second off the inside of the post. Substitute Peter Duffield added a third in injury time. He'd only been on the field for three minutes after replacing Nogan but he was on hand to meet a low right-wing cross from Liddle and turn it into the net.

From a game that had looked to be heading towards stalemate, the Quakers had hit three goals in the last seven minutes to secure a victory that, in fairness, probably flattered them, but none of the home supporters were complaining as Ian and I left the ground.

I thought that Andy Collett's save from Kieron Durkan actually won Darlington the match. If that had gone in, I honestly don't think there would have been the same outcome. Even now, I can remember the save; it was that good, as was Andy to be honest.

* * *

David Stockdale – Career Details

David Stockdale at the time of writing plays as a goalkeeper for York City, after signing for them from Sheffield Wednesday in June 2023.

The stopper commenced his career in the Huddersfield Town youth system before joining York in 2000, where he became a trainee in 2002. He made his first-team debut on the last day of the 2002/03 season and established himself in the team in 2004/05, but in 2006, following loan spells at Wakefield-Emley and Worksop Town, he was released. Stockdale moved to Darlington and in his second season he played in the play-offs. He signed for Premier League club Fulham for an undisclosed fee in 2008, but never became a regular, and spent several spells on loan to Football League clubs. He joined Brighton & Hove Albion, then of the Championship, in 2014, and helped them win promotion to the Premier League in his third season there. He turned down a new contract with Brighton and signed for Birmingham City in 2017, then in 2018/19 he had spells on loan at Southend United, Wycombe Wanderers and Coventry City.

He was called up to the full England squad earlier in his career, but remained uncapped.

My Memorable Match Involving David Stockdale

Shrewsbury Town v Darlington – 2007/08

I travelled to this match with my friends John Gray and Rob Marquiss in Ian's car.

Before we left Darlington I printed the route that we had to take and John kindly volunteered to keep Ian right.

Everything went swimmingly until John forgot to remind our driver to turn off the M6 and head towards Chester which meant we ended up going over 40 miles out of our way! I took great delight in taking the mickey out of the somewhat unfortunate John. Ian and Rob joined in which meant that our victim had little choice other than to laugh things off, which to his credit he did.

Once we had found the right way we quickly made up time and were at the stadium by quarter past six. I said to John that if he hadn't cocked up the route we'd have been there much quicker; he couldn't argue and responded by saying, 'Well we all make mistakes.' I told him that a 'full account' would go into any book that I wrote in the future. He simply laughed and said that it wouldn't be the first time he had been made to look a fool in my books and knowing me it probably wouldn't be the last! I couldn't really contest that point and with the winding up session now at an end the four of us headed to the supporters' bar where we had a sandwich and something to drink. Then we made our way to the away end to watch what was, in fairness, a mediocre performance from Darlington.

It was raining rather heavily so Rob, Ian and I took up the option to watch the match from a covered, elevated disabled area. I have to say the view was excellent from where we sat.

I was pleased to see that my friend and winger Neil Wainwright was back among the Darlington substitutes after he'd been left out of the final 16 that featured in the previous match, a defeat to Wycombe Wanderers. In all honesty I think he should have been in the team simply because he caused opposing full-backs problems with his pace. Unfortunately, this was my opinion, and not the manager's.

Darlington started slowly and had David Stockdale to thank for keeping the score sheet blank, especially in the early stages. Firstly in the sixth minute he went down at his near post to deny Ben Davies a goal, then shortly afterwards he punched away Marc Pugh's left-wing cross before any of the Shrewsbury forwards could take advantage. In the 32nd minute

Dave Penney's men created their first real chance of the match but Tommy Wright fired wide after Guylain Ndumbu-Nsungu, on for the hugely disappointing Kevin Gall, had headed the ball into his path. That was the last action in what was a poor Darlington display against what could only be described as an extremely weak Shrewsbury side.

The Quakers started the second half in much the same way as they had the first. One thing I noticed was that the players' movement off the ball was really poor, as was their passing, which left the visiting fans who were sitting next to me frustrated to say the least.

The closest Darlington came to scoring was midway through the second half when Stephen Foster got his head to Ben Parker's corner but the effort was cleared off the line by Shrewsbury's central defender Kelvin Langmead. A minute after that effort, Jason Kennedy shot wide from the edge of the penalty area. Wright did exactly the same as Kennedy when he fired wide from 18 yards after good work from Pawel Abbott, who had come on for Ndumbu-Nsungu. This meant that the Quakers had to be content with a point; it was one that they probably didn't deserve, but that happens sometimes in football, as any fan will tell you.

Without doubt, David Stockdale won Darlington that point. I mentioned this to Ian and he agreed with me as he pushed me out of the ground.

* * *

Peter Jameson – Career Details

Born in Sunderland, Peter Jameson firstly played youth football with Middlesbrough, where he was a 'training goalkeeper' for the first-team players.

Following his release from Middlesbrough, Peter played in non-league football for Consett and Sunderland Ryhope Community Association, before signing for Darlington in October 2013. He then moved on loan to South Shields in March 2017.

After 119 league and 12 cup appearances for Darlington, Jameson left by mutual consent in August 2017 and signed for Blyth Spartans. He stayed there for two years before moving to York City in June 2019 and later signing for Football League club Harrogate Town in May 2022. Peter spent 2023/24 on loan at Hartlepool United before rejoining Darlington in July 2024 following his release from the Sulphurites.

My Memorable Match Involving Peter Jameson
Darlington v Stourbridge – 2015/16

Despite not being very well (I was still suffering from the after effects of a serious car accident), I went to this match at Darlington's temporary home, Heritage Park in Bishop Auckland, with Ian in his car. We watched from the upstairs bar, from where we were afforded an excellent view.

The pair of us witnessed the Quakers make the perfect start, when within the first five minutes Stephen Thompson gave them the lead. The winger picked up a loose pass and drove at the visitors' defence before passing the ball into the corner of the net.

The rest of the half would prove to be a struggle for the makeshift home defence with Peter Jameson twice keeping Darlington ahead. He first smothered from Karl Hawley at the near post before making another smart stop shortly after. Leon Scott also made a goal-saving tackle when Jameson parried an effort, and Scott somehow prevented Hawley from tapping the ball home.

The equaliser was coming and it was Hawley who struck after 30 minutes when he easily finished after being played through on goal.

Lee Gaskell almost regained the lead for the home side, but his fierce volley went just over the top just before half-time.

The second period saw Scott move to the centre of defence with Anthony Callaghan going to left-back. The half was more even, but the hosts were again thankful for Jameson, as he made an excellent double save to deny one of the visiting forwards. Shortly after, Darlington right-winger Adam Mitchell had a strike from outside the box go just over the top of the bar.

Graeme Armstrong, who had come on midway through the half, came close to scoring with a header from a free kick late on, but it was the visitors who missed a glorious chance to win the game in stoppage time. Hawley was unmarked in the area, but was unable to direct his header on target as the game finished all square.

As Ian pushed me back to the car, I said that it had been an extremely poor performance and if it hadn't been for Peter Jameson, we wouldn't have even secured the point. He agreed and asked whether it had been worth me going through the pain barrier to get the match. My simple answer was, 'No.'

* * *

Tommy Taylor – Career Details

Tommy Taylor played in the youth teams at Sheffield Wednesday, before he joined Brighouse in 2011. He had a brief spell at Halifax Town in 2013 and then he moved on to Farsley for two seasons, where he won the Northern Premier League Division One North Player of the Year award.

He moved back to Brighouse for a second spell, before spending three seasons at Scarborough Athletic where he helped them win promotion from the NPL Division One North. He also had trials during this time at Rotherham United and Cambridge United. Unfortunately, these didn't lead to anything.

In the summer of 2020 he signed for another Northern Premier League club, Buxton, and played for them until the season was curtailed because of Covid.

Tommy signed for Darlington in May 2021. He played over 100 matches for the Quakers before being released at the end of the 2023/24 season. At the time of writing, Tommy has just signed for Worksop Town.

My Memorable Match Involving Tommy Taylor

Darlington v Newcastle United U23 – 2021/22

I watched this match from the comfort of my own home on Quaker TV.

Darlington settled well and showed one or two glimpses of good attacking play, while Newcastle had a goal ruled out for offside at the other end after Tommy Taylor had beaten away an effort down to his right. Darlington went close on 17 minutes when midfielder Will Hatfield curled a free kick over from the left for former Newcastle striker Luke Charman to glance just wide. Good, patient play on the left involving Hatfield, Joe Wheatley and Joey Hope ended with the latter playing the ball into the box for Charman to have a shot blocked by a defender a few yards out. On 25 minutes, Hope, who was finding plenty of space on the left flank, was picked out by Hatfield, and he struck a left-footed shot from the corner of the box that only just cleared the crossbar. A few minutes later, Hatfield had a penalty appeal turned down when he burst into the box and appeared to be tripped, but the referee waved play on. Newcastle took the lead on 38 minutes when midfielder Tom Allan controlled a long ball, got away from the Darlington defence and fired left-footed past Taylor's outstretched right hand.

The home side almost levelled when Joe Wheatley played a one-two with Charman and fired just wide from inside the area. That was the last meaningful action of what was an entertaining first half.

Newcastle put a brand new team on for the second half. The Quakers started really well and equalised on 53 minutes. Hatfield curled over a teasing free kick from the right to the far post, where the ball was bundled into the net, with defender Lexus Beeden claiming a touch. There was concern five minutes later when Taylor was caught by Newcastle striker Dylan Stephenson as he pushed away a right-wing cross, but he was able to resume after treatment. Youngster Lucas Martin, however, did come on for the goalkeeper on 67 minutes and his first taste of action was to save a low shot by Longelo.

The Magpies took the lead on 79 minutes after the ball was threaded through for Stephenson to slide past the advancing Martin. They made sure right at the end when the same player ran through and slipped his shot past the substitute.

As I turned my PC off, I thought about the game. Tommy Taylor had been really solid while he was on the pitch, and I was really impressed with him.

After the match, I contacted the club and sponsored Tommy's away shirt until he left at the end of the 2022/23 season. He's one of my favourite post-2012 players.

2

Defenders

Clive Nattress – Career Details

Clive Nattress made 340 appearances in the Football League playing in defence for Darlington and Halifax Town in the 1970s and 1980s. He also played for Consett, Blackpool (though not for the first team), as well as Northern League Bishop Auckland, Crook Town (as player-manager) and Ferryhill Athletic. While still a Darlington player, he took part as a guest in Crook's pioneering tour to India in 1976. Clive, during his career, played in every position for the Quakers, even goalkeeper!

Interestingly, Clive is a cousin of the former newsreader Angela Rippon.

My Memorable Match Involving Clive Nattress

Darlington v AFC Bournemouth – 1976/77

I went to this match with my mother. I was lucky that she let me take a week off from boarding school to attend.

The early signs weren't too promising for the home side when midfielder and former Manchester United player Eric Young injured his thigh with his first tackle of the night and had to hobble off. He had to be replaced by substitute Norman Lees, making his first appearance for seven months. Due to the lack of available players, Lees was only on the bench in case of emergencies but was faced with playing virtually the whole game.

Darlington didn't let Young's injury affect them, and they grabbed the lead in the fifth minute with a sweeping move. John Stone played a superb crossfield pass to Lees, who played the ball forward to Eddie Rowles. The striker beat two defenders down the right and crossed low and hard to Clive Nattress to fire home from six yards. The Quakers were playing some of their best football of the season and had the Bournemouth goal under constant pressure. Dave Crosson fired in a shot from 20 yards that visiting keeper Steve Chalk did well to hold. Shortly after, centre-forward Ron Ferguson just failed to connect as Nattress shot across goal. Chalk was in action again with a great save from a Derek Craig header but he was helpless after 26 minutes as Rowles increased the lead, blasting in a shot from 20 yards that struck both posts before going in. Minutes later, it was 3-0 as Nattress produced a brilliant run down the left which took him past three defenders before crossing to Steve Holbrook who steered home from eight yards out.

The second half could never maintain the frantic pace of the first, and although the visitors came more into the game, they never really looked like scoring and in fact it was Darlington who added a fourth goal in the last minute. Full-back Keith Miller brought down Steve Holbrook as he advanced into the box, and Bobby Noble stepped up to fire home the penalty to make the final score 4-0 to my beloved Quakers.

While my mother pushed me home, I revealed that I was pleased that she'd allowed me to talk her into letting me skive school to go to the match. I then added that it was the best I'd seen Clive Nattress play for the club. She smiled at my comment and then agreed that he'd been excellent, especially in the first half. I was certainly one happy little boy as we continued our journey.

* * *

Kevan Smith – Career Details

Kevan first appeared for his local team, Darlington. He was on trial in a game against the club's professionals under the then manager Len Walker before playing in the reserves against Barnsley shortly after.

In the summer of 1979, Walker left the Quakers but Smith was invited back by the newly appointed Billy Elliott. He impressed Elliott in the reserves and was quickly snapped up.

Kevan made his debut at Torquay United in September 1979 as the Quakers lost 4-0. Team-mate Clive Nattress called him 'Smudger'. It was a nickname which stuck with him for the rest of his time at the club. Smith turned out to be a brave, hard-working and committed player.

However it was under Elliott's successor, Cyril Knowles, that Smith really came into his own and by his own admission improved as a player. Knowles, who joined Darlington in 1983, demanded nothing less than 100 per cent from his players and Kevan filled the mould perfectly.

The 1984/85 season saw Darlington promoted from the Fourth Division, but the defender left for pastures new when he joined Rotherham United in 1985.

Kevan later moved to Coventry City for £65,000. Although he was a member of their squad when they won the FA Cup (he did not feature due to injury), he played only a handful of top-flight games for the Sky Blues, partly due to injury. He moved to York City in 1988 where things failed to work out, but by this stage Darlington and rivals Hartlepool United were interested in securing his services.

Smith rejoined Darlington, who had recently been relegated to the Conference, after speaking to Brian Little. Interestingly, in under a year, Smith had dropped from the top of English football to the bottom; having said that, his second spell at Darlington would prove to be the best years of his career.

Darlington won promotion from the Conference at the first attempt and the following season, 1990/91, they were promoted from the Fourth Division to the Third. Brian Little left to manage Leicester City and the bottom dropped out of Smith's world. The pair were very close and Little was begged to stay by the player. Little recommended Smith for the management job at the club but instead Smudger convinced Little's assistant, Frank Gray, to take the job.

Smith had felt he was too young for the role, but when Gray left the club in 1992 he did apply. However, Ray Hankin was given the position as a temporary measure. Kevan had hoped to get the job and had an interview, though the Quakers installed former Sheffield United coach Billy McEwan on a permanent basis. The pair's relationship was rocky at best. In the summer of 1992, the player required a major operation and was told he would need ten weeks to recover but came back after nine. Upon Smith's return, McEwan said he wanted a new central defender.

Matters remained difficult between the pair and later McEwan told Smith he was being released on a free transfer. By this stage though, Smith was close to a testimonial and refused to leave. The relationship between the pair got worse and Kevan was left further isolated and had to train on his own. Towards the end of his time at the club Smith did regain his place in the team. Between September 1997 and October 1998 Smith was joint manager of Northern League club Crook Town, working with former Darlington team-mate Paul Cross.

Smith returned to the Quakers to work for them as a Football in the Community officer and went on to be assistant manager at Hull City with his former manager and good friend, Brian Little.

After leaving the Tigers, Kevan set up his own cleaning business, which he still has at the time of writing.

My Memory of Kevan Smith

Firstly, I should explain that Kevan is a good friend of mine. I first met him in 1979 and we are still in touch to this day.

My main memory didn't happen on the football pitch. Let me explain.

In the 1980s I was working voluntarily with the Darlington supporters' club and despite being only 17, I arranged a stag night, with strippers, to both raise money and also to get the players together. My story covers the aftermath when I was summoned to then manager Billy Elliott's office to explain what had gone on.

A stern-faced Billy was sitting behind a large desk with me directly opposite him. I have to say, it was like being back at school. I tried not to smile as I thought of the time school friend Malcolm and I tried to run away and I ended up in the headmaster's office with my mother. I was brought back from my trance when I noticed Kevan gleefully watching the proceedings from a rear window, invisible to the manager.

After a few seconds, Billy looked at me and asked, 'So Paul, tell me, how old are you?' I hesitated, not quite sure whether to admit that I was actually under age, but thought it best to be honest so I responded by replying, 'I'm 17, boss.' Billy shook his head in disbelief and then stated in a raised voice, 'Seventeen! So you're not even old enough to drink, never mind organise this fiasco.' I put my head down before saying quietly, 'No, Billy.'

At this stage of my telling off, I was doing my utmost to avoid eye contact with Kevan who was now trying to get a reaction from me by grinning at me through the window. Billy attracted my attention by stating, again in a raised voice, 'Given your age, I can't believe you were responsible for hiring those bloody strippers.' I half smiled and said, 'I just thought it would be a bit of fun, boss.' Billy shook his head angrily and then in an even more raised voice stated, 'Fun! You reckon? Well I can tell you it certainly wasn't fun to have my bloody ear chewed off all day by the press.'

Once again, I was distracted by Kevan, who was still grinning at me. Unfortunately, on this occasion, I was no longer unable to contain myself and burst out laughing. Quite rightly, Billy was incensed and shouted, 'It's not funny, boy!' I tried my best to control myself and shook my head and responded by saying, 'No, Billy. I'm really sorry.' Billy paused for a few seconds and passed his 'sentence' by stating, 'Right. You're banned from the ground for one week and that includes matches. Get out of my sight and send Kevan in before I really lose my temper.'

Kevan and I still talk about that incident to this day and I have to say that it's an honour to have known him for all of my adult life.

* * *

Harry Wilson – Career Details

Harry Wilson was born in 1953 and began his club career as an apprentice with Burnley; it was as a Clarets player that he played for the England youth team in 1970/71.

With Burnley's relegation from the First Division already confirmed, Wilson made his first-team debut on 26 April 1971, aged just 17 years and five months, playing at left-back in a 1-0 win against Chelsea. He kept his place for the last match of the season, and made ten Second Division appearances in 1971/72, as one of four players tried at left-back, but the arrival of England international full-back Keith Newton from Everton meant Wilson played no part in Burnley's 1972/73 Second Division-winning campaign. Shortly after his 20th birthday, following 18 months of second-team football, Wilson and fellow long-term reserve team player Ronnie Welch were signed by Brian Clough for Brighton & Hove Albion for £70,000.

Harry went straight into their starting 11 and kept his place for two and a half seasons before being dislodged by Chris Cattlin, but still made 17 appearances for the 1976/77 Third Division promotion squad, taking his total to 146 appearances in all competitions.

In the 1977 close-season, Albion signed Mark Lawrenson and Gary Williams from Third Division club Preston North End, and supplied Wilson and Graham Cross in part exchange. Wilson played the first 23 matches of 1977/78, all but one in the starting 11, when a motor accident left him in hospital for several weeks. Suggestions that his career was over proved wrong and he returned at the beginning of the 1978/79 season in the Second Division, to which Preston had been promoted in his absence. After eight league starts, he fell out of contention, and the following season he made 12 league starts, the last of which was on 21 December 1979.

He was transfer-listed in February 1980, and a month into 1980/81 he signed for the then Fourth Division Darlington. The Quakers had been forced to apply for re-election the previous season after finishing in the bottom four and targeted Wilson to fill a vacancy at left-back and to add experience to a small and very young squad. He made 90 appearances over three years, a third of which was interrupted by injury, before finishing his Football League career with Hartlepool United. It would be a further 18 years before another player – Neil Aspin – made the same move on a permanent basis.

In 1984 Wilson moved into non-league football, first as a player with Crook Town of the Northern League and then as a manager, with fellow Northern League sides Seaham Red Star and Whitby Town. He went on to act as Sunderland's community officer, later coached at Burnley and Bury, and worked for the Football League monitoring clubs' youth systems in what had been an interesting and indeed varied career.

My Memorable Match Involving Harry Wilson
Darlington v Wigan Athletic – 1980/81

I sat in the East Stand Paddock with my mother where we witnessed the visitors have an early spell of sustained pressure which kept the home defence busy, but they were unable to trouble Darlington keeper Kevin Barry, Dave McMullen going closest when he headed wide. Darlington, however, weathered the early storm and took the lead in the 14th minute. New signing Harry Wilson played a perfect through ball to John Stalker who shrugged off a weak tackle by Neil Davids before shooting calmly across goalkeeper John Brown into the far corner of the net. The lead only lasted for ten minutes before the visitors drew level with a gifted equaliser when Dave McLean tried to steer a right-wing cross from David Fretwell out for a corner, but only succeeded in turning the ball inside his own post. Harry Charlton and Alan Walsh both went close as the home side pressed forward, but with Tommy Gore working well in midfield, the visitors were always a threat. Darlington finished the half well on top with three corners in quick succession but couldn't make the pressure tell.

Wigan started the second half strongly with substitute David Glenn hitting the angle of post and bar before McMullen missed the target from 12 yards when in the clear. Darlington hit back and regained the lead in the 77th minute. David Speedie played a brilliant through ball into the path of Stalker, who once again outstripped Davids before lobbing over the advancing Brown from an acute angle. Wigan recovered and Frank Corrigan squandered a great chance to equalise when he headed Gore's cross wide from only five yards out. Stalker sealed the victory in injury time when he completed his hat-trick with a fine solo goal. He turned Davids and Colin Methven on the edge of the visitors' box and fired towards goal. His shot was beaten out by Brown but Stalker snapped up the rebound to celebrate the first Feethams hat-trick since Eddie Rowles had put three goals past Scarborough in the FA Cup in 1976.

While Stalker stole all the headlines with his goals, Alan Kamara was the man of the match with an outstanding performance at right-back. New boy Wilson also had an impressive debut but unsurprisingly faded in the last 20 minutes due to a lack of match fitness. I have to say, I was super impressed with our new left-back. This was mentioned by me to my mother as she pushed me home from the ground. I often wonder now whether she ever got bored with my constant chattering about Darlington Football Club. I'll never know now as she's no longer with us, but she always seemed to listen and indeed remember what I'd said, even after a few weeks.

* * *

John Craggs – Career Details
John Craggs spent his entire playing career in the north-east of England. He played over 400 games for Middlesbrough but also had spells at Newcastle United and Darlington.

After a total of 52 league appearances at Newcastle, Middlesbrough paid a then club record £60,000 fee to bring the full-back to Teesside in 1971. After a testimonial match against Newcastle in the summer of 1982, Craggs left Middlesbrough to rejoin his former club before ending his playing days at Darlington. He took up a coaching role at Hartlepool after leaving the Quakers in 1985.

John is now happily retired at the time of writing.

My Memorable Match Involving John Craggs
Blackpool v Darlington – 1984/85

This match always reminds me of the quality the by then veteran full-back still had, despite almost being at the end of his brilliant playing career. By this time, John was player-coach and didn't play every match.

With it still being early in the season, my friend Stephen Lowson and I went to Blackpool on the train and were there well before the kick-off.

After going to a few pubs, which included lunch, the pair of us headed for Bloomfield Road, home of Blackpool Football Club.

We witnessed one of the most boring games one could imagine. Darlington manager Cyril Knowles had gone with the aim of taking a point home.

During the game, time after time, John Craggs passed the ball back to goalkeeper Fred Barber, who didn't even have to move to pick it up (goalkeepers could do that in those days). I honestly can't remember either team having a worthwhile shot. The Blackpool fans were going crazy, but Craggs had Blackpool in his back pocket. I have to say, it was one of the best displays I've seen from a defender and to this day, I've never forgotten it.

Stephen and I were over the moon with the point as we headed back to the train station.

* * *

Peter Johnson – Career Details

Peter Johnson played as a left-back. He made a total of 399 appearances in the Football League for Middlesbrough, Newcastle United (where he played with John Craggs, who he also played with at Middlesbrough and Darlington), Bristol City, Doncaster Rovers, Darlington, Crewe Alexandra, Exeter City, Southend United, Gillingham and Peterborough United. At Southend, he made over 120 appearances. In 1992, he moved to Wycombe Wanderers, at that time, still a non-league club.

My Memorable Match Involving Peter Johnson

Darlington v Northampton Town – 1984/85

I again went with Stephen. We saw Darlington make a bright start and grab the lead after only five minutes, Kevin Todd playing a delightful through ball into the path of Carl Airey who calmly slotted past Cobblers keeper Peter Gleasure for his first goal for the club. It was very nearly 2-0 five minutes later when Dave Hawker, Dave McLean and Mark Miller combined well to set up Colin Ross, but his first-time shot was turned around the post by Gleasure.

The Quakers kept up the pressure and it came as no surprise when the second goal arrived on 14 minutes. A Miller corner was missed by everyone in the goalmouth and ran through to the far post for John Hannah to drive home. The visitors tried hard to get back into the game but looked short on confidence in front of goal. They should have made more of an indirect free kick in the area after 32 minutes. Neil Brough squared the ball to Brian Mundee but his shot was blocked by goalkeeper Fred Barber and the ball was hacked clear following a goalmouth scramble.

Then just before half-time defender Russell Lewis missed the best chance of the game when he scooped the ball over the bar when it looked easier to score.

The second half began with the hosts comfortably in control and they added a third goal after 55 minutes. Miller was held back as he advanced towards the penalty area but the referee waved play on. When the tricky winger got into the box, he was tripped by Mundee and a penalty was awarded. McLean made no mistake from the spot, blasting home. Darlington made it four on 64 minutes when Hawker made progress down the right and fired in a cross-come-shot that bounced back off the post and was volleyed home from close range by Airey. Northampton had one last chance to get themselves on the score sheet on 76 minutes when Trevor Lee sent a free header wide, but they finished the game a well beaten side.

I can remember that Peter Johnson was up and down the left wing during the whole game and I was impressed by his energy levels as I left the ground.

* * *

Phil Lloyd – Career Details
Phil Lloyd was born in Hemsworth, in Yorkshire, and played as a central defender for Middlesbrough, Barnsley, Darlington, Torquay United and Devon non-league club Elmore.

He was part of Darlington's promotion squad in 1984/85 and was a fan favourite.

After retiring from football, Phil settled in the south-east of England where he still lives at the time of writing.

My Memorable Match Involving Phil Lloyd
Darlington v Middlesbrough, FA Cup third round replay – 1984/85
Three days after the original drawn tie at Ayresome Park, Darlington played Middlesbrough in the replay after 50 or so loyal fans had turned up to clear two inches of snow from the pitch. Because of the demand for tickets, Stephen, who took me to the game that night, had to stand in the Tin Shed and I had to go in one of the East Stand seats with a guy called Tom (not his real name) as my usual spot in the East Stand Paddock wouldn't have afforded much of a view with so many bodies in front of me.

Spurred on by a crowd of 14,237, both sides tried to play football on a treacherous bog of a pitch, but the first half ended in a goalless stalemate. However, things changed in the 53rd minute when Garry Macdonald managed to scramble the ball past the visiting goalkeeper Kelham O'Hanlon to put the Quakers 1-0 up. Feethams erupted. Cyril Knowles's men doubled their lead in the 76th minute; they won a corner, Mitch Cook crossed into the box and Mike Angus rolled the ball through the muddy goalmouth to Phil Lloyd who toe-poked it into the net. Once more there was uproar but this time the Middlesbrough fans invaded the pitch in a vain attempt to get the game abandoned. Play was held up for ten minutes and the referee made it clear that if necessary he would wait until midnight to finish the tie. I have to admit that the violence was pretty bad but the police managed to eventually bring it under control. Altogether there were 15 arrests and three people were taken to hospital. Concrete slabs and iron spikes were even hurled at the police after a 20-yard section of the perimeter fencing behind one of the goals collapsed.

After what seemed like an eternity, the game was restarted and Tony McAndrew almost instantly pulled a goal back for Boro. The Quakers therefore had to endure a frantic last ten minutes before the referee blew the final whistle. I was ecstatic with what was an outstanding victory.

I'll never forget Phil Lloyd's goal against his former club. Looking back now, this was probably because he didn't score many, so, that's probably why it stuck in my mind.

* * *

Gary Morgan – Career Details

Gary Morgan began his football career with hometown club Consett as a left-back before spending two seasons playing for Berwick Rangers in the Scottish Second Division.

In 1985, Gary returned to England to join the then Third Division Darlington for a £10,000 fee.

During his four years with the club, they were relegated twice. He left after the Quakers' second relegation, which took them into the Conference under Brian Little. He later played non-league football for Bishop Auckland in the Northern League.

My Memorable Match Involving Gary Morgan
Darlington v Swansea City – 1985/86

Ian and I were at Feethams to see Darlington make an impressive start. Their fast-moving attack was always on top and the visitors did well to hold out for 28 minutes until a favourable decision to the home side opened the floodgates. Gary Emmanuel was adjudged to have handled inside the box, when a clearance from one of his fellow defenders hit his arm, and Dave McLean made no mistake with the penalty. Darlington followed that up with two more quickfire goals. Firstly, Malcolm Poskett headed powerfully home from a Chris Evans cross, and then Alan Roberts broke from halfway before rounding visiting keeper and former England international Jimmy Rimmer and slotting home. Just before half-time McLean scored his second penalty of the game after a clumsy push on Gary Pallister by Alan Waddle, and then straight after the interval Garry MacDonald scored his fourth goal in three games with a fierce drive that gave Rimmer no chance.

Darlington had hit five goals in an 18-minute spell either side of the break. Swansea had a chance to reduce the arrears in the 51st minute when they were awarded a penalty of their own after a foul by Chris Evans, but Fred Barber brilliantly saved Colin Pascoe's spot-kick. He then made an even better save from the follow-up. Steve Tupling scored the final goal in the 87th minute with a fine solo effort.

As Ian took me home in his car, I can remember commenting that Gary Morgan had been a good summer signing and that his excellent defending certainly helped Darlington get the three points; his passing from the back was also top-notch. Ian agreed that Morgan had been very good during the match.

* * *

Gary Coatsworth – Career Details

Gary Coatsworth was born in Sunderland. After leaving school, he worked as a panel beater and played youth football locally. Two of his team-mates at Sunday league team Moorside, Lee Howey and Clive Mendonca, also went on to play professional football. In 1986, a trial with Second Division club Barnsley proved successful, and he accepted the offer of a contract.

Gary made his Football League debut on 19 December 1987 at home to Millwall. His team were 2-0 up when unfortunately his back-pass allowed the visitors' Teddy Sheringham to score, but in the end this didn't really matter as Barnsley went on to win 4-1. He did not return to the first team until the last few matches of the season, when he made three appearances as a substitute and two starts, but he played only reserve team football and at the end of the 1988/89 season he was released.

Coatsworth signed for Darlington, newly relegated to the Conference but managed by the ambitious Brian Little. Initially unable to displace Les McJannet from the full-back position, he finally made his debut in November 1989; he broke a collarbone and was out for six weeks. By the last match of the season, away to Welling United, Darlington needed a draw to ensure promotion back to the Football League, whatever result was achieved by rivals Barnet. They had injury problems in defence, so Coatsworth came into the side and, with four minutes left and the match still goalless, he met a free kick with a header that looped over the goalkeeper and secured a 1-0 win.

He began the new Fourth Division season as a reserve, starting twice in October when McJannet and David Corner were unavailable and a further twice in similar circumstances in December; he scored his first Football League goal with a powerful header in a 3-1 defeat away to Stockport County. The last of his 12 league appearances was in the final match of the campaign, from which Darlington needed and achieved a win against Rochdale to secure a second successive title.

Brian Little left for Leicester City in May 1991 and after finally becoming a regular in Darlington's starting 11, Coatsworth followed him to the Second Division club in October for a £15,000 fee.

Gary made his first league start on 30 November in a 2-1 win away to Derby County, and performed well enough to keep his place for the next match, during which he was substituted with what was reported as a jarred knee. Minor surgery and specialist rehabilitation failed to fix the problem, and a second operation – nearly three months after the original injury – confirmed a ruptured cruciate ligament. It was another year before he returned to the first team, but his return marked the start of a winning run that included his first goals for Leicester – a header and an angled drive with three minutes left to complete a 3-2 win away to former club Barnsley – and pushed the team into the play-off positions for a second year in a row. Unfortunately, Gary was unfit for the play-off final, having put a premature end to his season by playing on an already injured ankle.

He signed a two-year contract in July 1993, but injured a hamstring in pre-season, and his only appearance in the first few months of the new season was as a substitute in the Anglo-Italian Cup in September. He came into the side in December, and for the first time in his Leicester career he was able to retain a regular place. His 25-yard volley opened the scoring in a 2-1 defeat of Luton Town that helped Leicester reach the play-offs for a third consecutive year. He scored again in the last regular-season match, a draw with Wolverhampton Wanderers. Coatsworth was in the Leicester team that faced Derby in the play-off final at Wembley. Derby went in front in the first half then a few minutes before half-time the referee Roger Milford missed Iwan Roberts's foul on Derby's goalkeeper Martin Taylor, while a covering defender missed Steve Walsh's weak header on the goal line and the scores were tied. Walsh scored again late in the game, and Leicester were promoted to the Premier League.

Gary was not included among the players named by Little as those he expected to use in the opening weeks of the 1994/95 Premier League season. He continued for a few months in the reserves, until, in February 1995, he confirmed his retirement. Because of the club's injury problems at the end of the previous season, Gary had played on despite a cyst that caused severe swelling in his ankle after matches. Removal did not fix the problem, and a surgeon told him that he had arthritis which would lead to serious mobility issues in later life if he continued to play professional football.

Coatsworth returned to his native Sunderland, where he took a job at the Nissan car plant. Before the end of the season, he was playing for Spennymoor United of the Northern Premier League Premier Division; he later played for Washington Nissan in the Wearside League, helping them win the title in 2001, and appeared for them in the Northern League. He eventually gave up the game because it was incompatible with his paid work. At the time of writing, he was still working at Nissan, employed as a supervisor.

My Memorable Match Involving Gary Coatsworth
Welling United v Darlington – 1989/90

The final match of the 1989/90 season was Welling United away in May 1990, which would be a truly nail-biting affair as Darlington needed a victory in order to secure promotion back to the Football League at the first attempt.

We set off from Darlington early on Saturday morning. There were three of us in the car that day: Ian, a lad called Graham Dixon from Bishop Auckland, and me. When we arrived in London at about midday we dropped the car off outside my friend Stephen Lowson's house in Bounds Green and then caught a southbound train across the Thames to Welling, where we met up in a pub with fellow Darlington fans Trevor Rutter, Brian Elsey and Phil Rutter.

Well over 1,000 visiting supporters packed into the away end of the leafy Park View Road Ground that day.

There was a carnival mood among them and some had entered into the spirit of the occasion by wearing fancy dress, such as a clown's outfit, while a veteran fan called Brian (sadly now no longer with us) even turned up sporting his kilt.

To cap it all it was a scorching day, with temperatures well into the 80s, the pitch was bone hard and the away fans were exposed to the baking sun, since the ground largely consisted of open terracing.

But what an unforgettable experience it was! We got there early and the atmosphere was absolutely brilliant. The game wasn't a particularly good spectacle from a purist's point of view, but the meaning of it was more important than the match itself.

With only three minutes remaining, Paul Emson was brought down by a clumsy late tackle on the left wing. Andy Toman cleverly swung in a cross to the far side of the penalty area where substitute Gary Coatsworth rose unchallenged to send a looping header past former Crystal Palace goalkeeper Paul Barron. It was his first senior goal.

I went wild as the whole of the away end erupted. We had achieved promotion back to the Football League, having been relegated the previous season. Words couldn't explain my exhilaration when this was confirmed at the final whistle. 'We are back in the big time,' I thought as I was pushed out of the ground, more than an hour after the final whistle had been blown.

Even to this day, I smile when I think back to Gary's goal as it was and remains one of the highlights of my 50 years supporting the Quakers.

* * *

David Corner – Career Details

Born in Sunderland, David Corner joined his hometown club in 1984 at the age of 18. After Shaun Elliott suffered an injury during the 1984/85 season, David was able to establish himself in the team and was named in the starting line-up for the 1985 League Cup Final against Norwich City in only his fifth appearance. However, his mistake led to the only goal of the game when he was caught in possession by John Deehan, before the ball fell to Asa Hartford whose shot deflected in off Gordon Chisholm to seal a victory for the Canaries. He later played for Cardiff City, Peterborough United, Leyton Orient, Darlington (where he won two successive promotions) and Gateshead.

After retiring from football, David joined the police force.

My Memorable Match Involving David Corner
Darlington v Burnley – 1990/91

I witnessed the return of league football at Feethams with Ian. We saw the Quakers begin the game in determined fashion but they found visiting keeper Chris Pearce in superb form behind his overrun defence. The deadlock was broken on 28 minutes when the home side took the lead with a dubious penalty. Paul Emson crossed from wide on the left towards the far post where centre-forward John Borthwick challenged for the high ball with Burnley defenders Ian Bray and Andy Farrell. The referee spotted an offence that no one else had seen and pointed to the spot. Not one to look a gift horse in the mouth, Frank Gray gave Pearce no chance whatsoever with the resulting penalty.

Unfortunately, the lead lasted just seven minutes though as the visitors hit back to equalise. A short corner was played into the box by Bray and fired towards goal by Joe Jakub where centre-forward Ron Futcher was in the right place at the right time to hook the ball into the roof of the net from six yards out. The fast and furious pace continued and Darlington regained the lead on the stroke of half-time. A free kick on the halfway line was floated forward by Gray. Pearce left his line and came through a crowd of players to punch clear. His clearance was met by former Middlesbrough midfielder Gary Gill, 20 yards out, who superbly volleyed the ball back over the stranded keeper and his helpless defenders and into the net.

The visitors started the second half looking for an equaliser and Mark Prudhoe pulled off a spectacular save at point-blank range to deny Jakub. The Quakers needed a third goal to feel safe and it duly arrived on 55 minutes. Another Gray free kick was flicked on by Borthwick to David Cork, who rolled the ball across the face of the penalty area to the onrushing Les McJannet. The right-back smashed a first-time shot just inside the near post from the corner of the box with Pearce helpless. Burnley worked hard to get back into the game but the Darlington defence, superbly marshalled by Kevan Smith and David Corner, held firm and the few chances that were created fell to Futcher, who was having an off day in front of goal. In addition he was well marked by Corner, who left the former Luton Town player clearly frustrated by the end of the match.

* * *

Les McJannet – Career Details

Les McJannet made 193 appearances in the Football League playing as a right-back for Mansfield Town, Scarborough and Darlington between 1979 and 1992. He remained with Darlington for their 1989/90 Conference title-winning season and also played non-league football for clubs including King's Lynn, Burton Albion (many years before they reached the Football League), Matlock Town and Boston United.

Les also went on to manage in the non-league game, taking charge of Sutton Town, Glapwell and Carlton Town.

My Memorable Match Involving Les McJannet
Darlington v Cardiff City – 1990/91

I went to this match with Ian, despite the absolutely atrocious weather. Strong winds and heavy rain made for difficult playing conditions but the Quakers certainly adapted to the Feethams mud bath far better than their opponents, making light of the sticky pitch and starting the game with some enterprising football. They opened the scoring on 14 minutes when David Cork held the ball up well on the edge of the box before rolling it into the path of the onrushing Les McJannet. The full-back ran on a couple of strides into the penalty area and thumped a low drive beyond Roger Hansbury's despairing dive.

Cardiff hit back and Cohen Griffith hit a low shot that skidded off the wet turf, but Mark Prudhoe went full length to keep it out. It was to be Prudhoe's only anxious moment of the half as the home side took complete control. Cork made it 2-0 in the 37th minute with a superb finish. Exchanging passes with John Borthwick down the left, the striker found himself on the corner of the penalty area and cleverly chipped the ball across Hansbury into the far top corner of the net. It was 3-0 six minutes later as Prudhoe used the wind to launch a prodigious goal kick deep into the Cardiff half, where it was misjudged by the visiting defenders and allowed to bounce into the penalty area. Jim Willis met it, sticking out a long leg to loop the ball over the stranded keeper. The Quakers, three goals to the good and with the game already won, left the pitch at half-time to a rousing ovation.

They should have made it four early in the second half when Cork and Borthwick both had close-range shots kicked off the line. Play briefly switched to the other end where Mark Taylor thought he'd pulled a goal back, but his shot was brilliantly steered around the post by Andy Toman with Prudhoe beaten. Darlington continued to hold the upper hand, despite playing into the wind and rain, and Gary Gill went close with a shot, when a square ball to Cork may have been the better option. Darlington scored the fourth goal that their play deserved in the 64th minute after a foul on Toman. Drew Coverdale's inch-perfect free kick was met by a thumping Willis header. Hansbury did well to keep that out but could only watch as Mick Tait hit the rebound into the empty net. Cardiff scored a consolation goal three minutes from time when Griffith, their best player, turned home a left-wing cross from close range to deny Prudhoe a clean sheet.

Les McJannet's opening goal was discussed by Ian and I on our way to the pub; it was certainly 'a cracker', to use Ian's words.

* * *

Jim Willis – Career Details

Born in Liverpool, Jim Willis served his apprenticeship at Blackburn Rovers, before he signed for Halifax Town in 1986. His impact there and indeed at subsequent club Stockport County was limited, although he came into his own at Darlington where he won medals for both the Conference and Fourth Division titles despite suffering from a broken leg against Telford United in 1991. Willis's form at Feethams netted him a £250,000 move to Leicester City in late 1991, when he followed former Quakers manager Brian Little to Filbert Street.

He initially struggled at the higher level and was even loaned out to Bradford City at one stage. Eventually, however, Willis adapted to his new surroundings and this was verified when he was the man of the match in the play-off final of 1994 as Leicester secured promotion. In 1996, Jim was set to join Burnley but the deal collapsed at the last minute because of contractual problems. However, a year later, the defender was forced to retire from the game because of injury.

Jim did hope to become a manager, and had a brief spell in charge of Northern Premier League club Bamber Bridge. He was appointed in November 2001 but left after only two months because of Bamber Bridge's financial problems.

My Memorable Match Involving Jim Willis

AFC Bournemouth v Darlington – 1991/92

An away trip to Bournemouth was our first match of the 1991/92 season and with it being a long journey, Ian and I made the decision to go to this particular fixture on the supporters' club coach.

We left at five o'clock in the morning and we were there for around 12.30pm with one stop en route at Tamworth services. I remember that we had our breakfast there, all washed down with a pot of tea. Unfortunately, to our horror, we noticed cigarette ash floating in our cups after Ian had poured the tea! He therefore took the teapot back to the counter. Given that we didn't have time to drink the replacement, because the coach was about to leave, we decided to tip the remains of our meal into it in order that they couldn't recycle the contents! Was that childish? It probably was. However, it made me smile as we watched the woman who was clearing our table shake her head in our direction as we left.

Once in Bournemouth, we went to a pub, the name of which escapes me, and there were quite a few Darlington fans already in there. One of them was drunkenly trying to play the piano and the lads with him were attempting to sing along, which was actually quite funny to watch. It reminded me of a very poor karaoke act!

Leaving the drunken pianist and his cohorts behind, we had a few more drinks in Bournemouth's supporters' club, after which we proceeded to the match. I watched the game from the disabled area with Ian. Since the area was on slope, a steward put some wooden blocks under my wheels to stop my wheelchair from shooting down the incline. They certainly did the job, meaning that my wheelchair didn't move an inch.

The Quakers started off the way they had finished the previous season and won the game 2-1 with Jim Willis scoring the winner after Alec Watson, the Bournemouth and former Liverpool defender had put through his own goal.

During our long journey home, Ian and I discussed what a good game Jim had and that he'd richly deserved his goal. That was certainly a nice thought as I drifted off to sleep in my seat.

* * *

Frank Gray – Career Details

Frank Gray played for Leeds United, Nottingham Forest, Sunderland and Darlington (he won two successive promotions with the Quakers in 1989/90 and 1990/91), and he also won 32 Scotland caps.

He later managed Darlington, Farnborough Town, Grays Athletic, Woking, Basingstoke Town and Bashley.

At the time of writing Frank lives in Australia where he works as a pundit for Fox Sport Australia's Premier League coverage. In 2016, he worked in an advisory capacity for Manly United where he oversaw their junior programme and worked with their women's teams across all grades.

As well as being the younger brother of Eddie, interestingly Frank has several other football connections within his family.

His son Andy, a striker, came through the ranks at Leeds United and later played for Nottingham Forest, Preston, Oldham Athletic, Bradford City, Sheffield United, Sunderland, Burnley, Charlton Athletic and Barnsley. He also won two full international caps for Scotland. Frank's nephew Stuart played for Celtic and Reading as a full-back.

Finally, his grandson Archie, son of Andy, plays for Tottenham Hotspur at the time of writing, having joined them from Leeds in 2024.

My Memorable Match Involving Frank Gray

Darlington v Hartlepool United – 1991/92

Although Frank Gray didn't play in this match, in my opinion this was the highlight of his fairly short stint as Darlington manager.

I attended this early kick-off with Ian. The Quakers kicked off with a strong wind at their backs and made all the early running. Their first real attack came on six minutes when a Mitch Cook free kick was flicked on by Kevan Smith to debutant Dugald McCarrison, on loan from Celtic, who very nearly introduced himself to Darlington fans in spectacular fashion, but his overhead kick just cleared the crossbar. Four minutes later, Darlington were in front. Les McJannet played a crossfield ball into the path of former England international Nick Pickering; his run and cross from the left was inch perfect for Lee Ellison, arriving at the far post, to smash the ball first time past visiting keeper Martin Hodge.

McCarrison then had a good chance to increase the lead when he broke clear, but the ball bobbled and he lobbed over the bar. Andy Toman was the next to threaten when he robbed Ian Bennyworth but flicked his shot just wide of the near post.

It was all Darlington and they went further in front in the 15th minute with an own goal by John McPhail. A clearance by Hodge was headed back towards goal by Smith to McPhail who attempted a volleyed back-pass to his keeper, but he hit the ball far too well from 25 yards out and watched in horror as it beat Hodge and curled inside his left-hand post.

The hosts continued to pile forward and Toman had a goal disallowed on 21 minutes after a McCarrison handball. They weren't to be denied though and scored a third goal after 39 minutes. A long clearance by Pickering was completely misjudged by Bennyworth and McCarrison took full advantage, racing clear from the halfway line and coolly beating the advancing Hodge from the edge of the penalty area, threading his shot low inside the far post. There was still time for McCarrison to be denied by Hodge's foot and for Kevan Smith to twice go close to a fourth goal for the home side before the referee brought a one-sided first half to a close.

An angry visiting manager Alan Murray (later to manage Darlington) made both his substitutions at half-time, bringing on David McCreery and Ricardo Gabbiadini. The changes lifted the visitors who made more of a fight of it in the second period. The on-loan Johnson, comfortably Pools' best player, forced Mark Prudhoe into action, producing a full-length save to turn a shot around his left-hand post. Paul Olsson should have done better when he shot wide after 70 minutes, and then Gabbiadini fired high over the bar from ten yards out. Pools never really looked like getting back into the game though and Darlington wrapped up a convincing victory with their fourth goal after 84 minutes. Mick Tait chested down a long clearance from Hodge and fed the ball to McJannet. He swept it down the right wing to Smith who hooked over a long cross to Ellison at the far post. The young striker coolly controlled the ball and picked his spot before blasting into the net for his seventh goal in his last five games.

Unsurprisingly, Frank Gray was delighted with the 4-0 win and hailed it as the best performance of the season and the best during his stint as manager. His young strike force of Lee Ellison and Dugald McCarrison, quite rightly, took all the plaudits.

I couldn't argue with Frank's assessment as Ian pushed me to the pub for a celebration pint.

* * *

Sean Gregan – Career Details

Sean Gregan was born in Guisborough, in the North Riding of Yorkshire. He started his career with Darlington's youth system before signing a professional contract on 20 January 1991. He played for them for five years before joining Preston North End, being signed by Gary Peters on 29 November 1996 for £350,000. He captained Preston North End to the Second Division title.

Gregan signed for newly promoted Premier League club West Bromwich Albion on 3 August 2002 on a four-year contract for a fee of £2m. He made his debut against Manchester United at Old Trafford on 17 August. Sean scored his first goal for the club in a 1-0 home win over Southampton on 14 September, after goalkeeper Paul Jones failed to hold on to his 40-yard shot. Despite being a regular in the team, Gregan was unable to prevent the Baggies' relegation from the Premier League, but in 2003/04 he was instrumental in captaining the team to promotion back to the Premier League at the first attempt, before joining Leeds United in September 2004.

Due to a lack of first-team football in the 2006/07 season, Gregan was sent on loan on 8 November 2006 to Oldham Athletic of League One until 1 January 2007. He scored three days later on his debut, in a 4-3 win over Kettering Town in the FA Cup.

The defender left Leeds on 5 January 2007 after reaching an agreement over the remainder of his contract, and signed a two-and-a-half-year deal at Oldham Athletic three days later. His performance in their 3-0 win away to Walsall on 22 September 2007 earned him a place in the League One Team of the Week.

He was released by Oldham manager Dave Penney after being deemed surplus to requirements on 12 May 2009. However, Penney had a change of heart after being impressed with Gregan's attitude and fitness levels, and he was soon brought back to the club on a one-year contract. He was later made captain and remained a key feature in defence alongside Reuben Hazell.

Oldham player-manager Paul Dickov stated in October 2010 that he would allow Sean to leave the club, after he was unable to force his way into the team following an injury at the beginning of the 2010/11 season, so the player decided to join then Conference Premier club Fleetwood Town on 19 October 2010 on a three month loan. He left Oldham on 6 January 2011 after having his contract terminated and signed for Fleetwood permanently, before he was released at the end of 2010/11.

Gregan signed for Northern Premier League Premier Division club Kendal Town on 10 August 2011. He made his debut three days later when starting a 3-0 home win over Worksop Town, but suffered a ruptured achilles tendon on his second appearance, on 21 August against Matlock Town.

Sean returned to Darlington on 4 June 2012 as a player-coach, as part of new manager Martin Gray's backroom staff. He was appointed as joint manager, alongside Brian Atkinson, on 1 October 2017 for the rest of the 2017/18 season after Gray left for National League North rivals York City However, the two left four days later without having taken charge of a single match. With Atkinson also being a director of the Martin Gray Football Academy (MGFA), Football Association rules meant he was unable to hold the Darlington managerial position as the academy's owner was in charge at another club. Gregan turned down the offer of a six-month contract to take over as manager as he would have also had to relinquish his own role with the MGFA.

He joined Gray at York City in December 2017 as a part-time defensive coach, before taking up the full-time position of assistant manager in July 2018, but left on 19 August along with Gray.

My Memorable Match Involving Sean Gregan
Darlington v Lincoln City – 1995/96

Ian and I were there to see the Quakers go close twice in the opening few minutes, firstly through Simon Shaw's right-footed drive and then with Gary Bannister's first-time volley after a clever flick by Robbie Blake. Matt Carmichael drove a free kick through the Lincoln wall but straight at visiting keeper Barry Richardson and the home side grabbed the lead that their early play deserved in the 21st minute. Steve Gaughan picked up a pass from Matty Appleby 30 yards out. He sidestepped a defender and unleashed an absolute screamer into the top corner of the net, leaving Richardson helpless. The lead lasted for only three minutes as a right-wing corner by Jason Minett was headed home by Dutchman Gijsbert Bos for the equaliser. The hosts continued to push men forward, Sean Gregan the next to try his luck, but Richardson made a good save to keep him out.

Darlington regained the lead on the half hour. Blake received the ball from a throw-in and made progress down the left wing. He reached the byline and pulled the ball back for Gaughan to side-foot a simple second. The Quakers continued to dominate with Richardson just managing to punch away a Robbie Painter shot, then full-back Terry Fleming came to his keeper's rescue by clearing a Blake piledriver off the line.

In the 55th minute, completely against the run of play, Lincoln found another equaliser. Again it was a right-wing corner that caused the problem. The home defence failed to clear and in the goalmouth scramble that followed, Bannister's attempted clearance rebounded off Gareth Ainsworth and into the net.

Straight from the restart Darlington regained the lead. Blake, Bannister and Painter gathered around the kick-off and worked the ball forward in neat triangles. The move finished with Painter in possession down the right-hand side of the penalty area. He beat two defenders and crossed for Blake to calmly slot the ball home from six yards out. Less than a minute after being pegged back to 2-2, the home side were back in front, and this time they didn't let their lead slip. The Imps threw men forward looking for a third equaliser but the Quakers' defence held firm, despite having to deal with a succession of corners and long throws from the direct, route one approach of the Imps, with Sean Gregan particularly impressive.

* * *

Andy Crosby – Career Details

Andy Crosby was a central defender during his playing days. He began his career at Leeds United, but made his debut in the Football League after joining Doncaster Rovers in July 1991. He spent two and a half seasons with Rovers, before moving on to Darlington in December 1993 following a brief loan spell with Halifax Town. He played 211 games for Darlington in a stay which lasted almost five years. He spent the 1998/99 season with Chester City and was sold to Brighton & Hove Albion for £10,000 in July 1999, helping the Seagulls to win the Third Division title in 2000/01 before joining Oxford United on a free transfer in December 2001. He was named in the PFA's Third Division Team of the Year for 2003/04 and moved on a free transfer to Scunthorpe United in June 2004. He spent six seasons with the Iron, winning three promotions: from League Two in 2004/05, with the League One title in 2006/07 and via the League One play-offs in 2009. Crosby made 715 league and cup appearances during his 20-year playing career, scoring 43 goals.

He joined the backroom staff at Scunthorpe United and would follow manager Nigel Adkins to Southampton, Reading, Sheffield United and Hull City. During his time at Southampton, the club would win successive promotions from League One into the Premier League in 2010/11 and 2011/12. He served as the caretaker manager of the Northern Ireland under-21 team in 2020 and joined the coaching staff at Port Vale in March 2021. He served as their acting manager during Darrell Clarke's absence in the latter half of the 2021/22 season and became interim manager following Clarke's sacking in April 2023.

My Memorable Match Involving Andy Crosby
Darlington v Lincoln City – 1996/97

Ian and I were sitting in our usual place to see the Quakers make a good start, taking control very early on. Simon Shaw was twice unlucky not to open the scoring, firstly with a raking right-footed shot that visiting keeper Barry Richardson saved at full stretch, then with a 25-yard curler that flew just wide of the far post. Striker Robbie Blake then fired just over before the game burst into life with a three-goal blast in a five-minute spell. Michael Oliver opened the scoring for the Quakers in the 24th minute. Good work down the left by Blake and Darren Roberts created the space for Oliver to advance into the box and smash his shot into the top corner of the net past the helpless Richardson.

A minute later Oliver turned provider as he broke into the box again, this time squaring the ball back across goal for Russell Kelly to side-foot past Richardson from the edge of the box.

Three minutes later it was 3-0, Mark Barnard crossing from the left towards the far post where Roberts volleyed home from eight yards out. Lincoln pushed four men up front in the second half in an attempt to get back into the game, but it was the home side who increased their lead in the 75th minute with a fine individual goal by Roberts. Running into the box to get on to the end of another Oliver pass, he turned defender Kevin Austin inside out before crashing his shot past Richardson at the keeper's near post. Lincoln briefly threatened to get back into the game as the Quakers took their foot off the pedal, and scored two goals in three minutes. On 80 minutes, Tepi Moilanen got down well to make a save after a free kick but could only parry the ball to Gareth Ainsworth who fired home from close range, and then three minutes later Ainsworth was on hand again to slot home after Moilanen had completely misjudged a high ball into the box. The hosts completed the scoring in the 89th minute. Oliver broke away down the left and played in defender Phil Brumwell, who coolly controlled the ball and slotted past Richardson for his first league goal for the club.

I have to say that Andy Crosby played very well at the back for Darlington and successfully helped his team stand up against a second half Lincoln City onslaught.

* * *

Adam Reed – Career Details

Adam Reed played in the Football League as a defender for Darlington, where he started and ended his career. During his first spell he was voted both the supporters' and players' player of the season in 1994/95. A close-season move to Blackburn Rovers for a fee of £200,000 followed when he became their first signing after they were crowned Premier League champions. During his three years at Ewood Park his only first-team appearance was on the bench as a substitute in a League Cup game at Preston. He had loan spells at Darlington and Rochdale before returning to Feethams permanently on a free transfer.

After being released at the end of the 2003 season he spent a year at Whitby Town prior to his retirement.

Adam currently works at Middlesbrough FC as their first team physiotherapist as of the time of writing.

My Memorable Match Involving Adam Reed
Darlington v Swansea City – 1998/99

As Ian and I entered the newly built East Stand at Feethams, we both quickly noticed that the atmosphere in the ground was quite subdued considering our league position at that time. The Swansea City fans, by contrast, were much more boisterous and sang 'One nil to the sheep shaggers' after they scored their first goal, which brought a smile to my face, though the fact that they had scored did not amuse me in the slightest. Former Darlington striker and record signing Nick Cusack was in the Swansea team that day. He had played for the club for less than a season following his move from Motherwell for £95,000 in 1991.

Despite the odd atmosphere, the Quakers played well in patches and earned a 2-2 draw with goals from man of the match Adam Reed and former Leeds and Sheffield United striker Carl Shutt, two minutes into injury time

Speaking of Adam Reed, I have to say, it was good to see him wearing a Darlington shirt again, having been sold to Blackburn Rovers for £200,000 three years previously and after being farmed out to Rochdale and back to Darlington on loan, as mentioned earlier. He returned to Feethams on a free transfer – good business on the part of David Hodgson if you ask me! He was certainly impressive in this match.

* * *

Mark Barnard – Career Details

Mark Barnard was originally a forward who converted to left wing-back or left-back. An attack-minded left-sided player with an excellent left foot, his fitness was among the best in the wing-back position during the time he played.

Barnard, aka 'Barney', started his career back in July 1994 with Rotherham United as a trainee. After failing to make it into the first team setup, he moved on to Worksop Town.

After impressing during his time with the Tigers, Mark earned a move to Darlington, where he then went on to make 171 league and cup appearances and scored four goals for the club.

Four seasons later saw Barnard join Doncaster Rovers, before moving on to Northwich Victoria. During this period Barnard made two appearances for England C, scoring one goal.

Barnard later went back to Worksop, before heading for Tamworth, another spell at Northwich, Alfreton Town and Belper Town.

My Memorable Match Involving Mark Barnard

Darlington v Burnley – FA Cup first round 1998/99

The first round of the FA Cup provided the Quakers with a home tie against Second Division Burnley. However, the Feethams pitch was totally unplayable. With this in mind, our neighbours Middlesbrough stepped forward and kindly offered use of the Riverside Stadium to host the match – a generous gesture by their chairman Steve Gibson. It took place on Tuesday, 17 November. I made the short journey to Teesside with Ian in his car.

A crowd of 5,059 were in attendance and they saw Darlington make a strong start, forcing four corners in the first quarter of an hour with Glenn Naylor going closest to a goal with a header from one of them that went just wide. Burnley seemed quite happy to soak up the pressure and rely on counterattacks and it nearly paid off in the 16th minute when their most dangerous player, Glen Little, beat two men with a strong run but his enticing cross was cut out by Mark Barnard who conceded a corner. Two minutes later Marco Gabbiadini went close with a shot from the edge of the box that visiting keeper Frank Petter-Kval did well to save and then a minute later he made an even better save from a Gabbiadini header. Burnley hit back and Steve Morgan clipped the bar with a header from a Little corner. At the end of the half it was Darlington who threatened when Darren Roberts forced his way into the box but had his shot blocked by Petter-Kval. However, the deadlock was broken in the 37th minute when the visitors grabbed the lead. Quakers centre-half Steve Tutill lost the ball on the halfway line and it fell to Burnley full-back Phil Eastwood, who played the ball forward for former Middlesbrough striker Andy Payton to advance and easily beat David Preece.

Darlington began the second half in determined fashion. Brian Atkinson had a shot deflected wide and then Gabbiadini fired high over when in a good position. Burnley thought they'd increased their lead in the 53rd minute when Payton netted again but this time it was ruled out for offside. The striker was booked for disputing the decision. They did however make it 2-0 two minutes later with a controversial penalty when Payton went down under a challenge from Craig Liddle just inside the box. The referee saw nothing wrong and waved play on, but his assistant flagged and a penalty was awarded. Payton smashed home the resulting spot-kick.

The Quakers kept pressing forward; striker Mario Dorner replaced defender Gary Bennett and very nearly scored with his first touch, a right foot shot that just cleared the bar. Atkinson then hit a powerful shot which was blocked and Naylor followed up but Petter-Kval somehow scrambled his effort around the post. However, the game changed in the 73rd minute. Liddle played a back-pass to Preece and as he cleared the ball Payton went in late on the keeper and earned his second booking. Although two goals up, Burnley had to play the last 17 minutes with ten men, and Darlington got back into the game in the 80th minute. Naylor was pushed in the back by Brian Reid as they contested a cross from Michael Oliver and Atkinson coolly converted the resulting penalty. The Quakers were completely on top now and Burnley were hanging on for their lives. Dorner's chip went just over the bar then Gabbiadini blazed another shot too high, but in the 86th minute they got a deserved equaliser. A cross from the right by Gabbiadini was headed into the box by Oliver, touched back by Naylor and smashed into the net by Dorner from 12 yards out.

Adam Reed had a header cleared off the line and then as the game entered stoppage time, Darlington grabbed a dramatic winner. Oliver won a tackle 30 yards out and the ball ran to Dorner just outside the penalty area. He squared it to the corner of the box where the onrushing Mark Barnard hit a first-time shot across the keeper just inside the far post. From two down with ten minutes left Darlington had fought back to secure a famous victory.

Ian and I couldn't believe what we had just witnessed as we made our way back home, and we were pleased that we'd been present to see an absolutely fantastic performance from our team.

All I could talk about during our journey home was Mark Barnard's excellent match-winning goal.

* * *

Neil Aspin – Career Details

Neil Aspin was a solid defender who could play at centre-half and right-back. He was a good marker and an adept tackler. He made his debut in the Football League for Leeds United at the age of 16 in February 1982, which would be his only appearance in the First Division. He spent seven seasons in the Second Division with the club, making 244 league and cup appearances and being named as the club's player of the year for the 1984/85 season. He was sold to Port Vale for a £150,000 fee in July 1989 and would go on to make 410 appearances in all competitions during a ten-season stay at Vale Park. He was named as the club's player of the year in 1989/90 and helped the Valiants to win the Football League Trophy in 1993. The following season, 1993/94, he was named in the PFA Team of the Year as he helped Vale to win promotion out of the Second Division. As well as this, Neil again won the Port Vale player of the year award. He also played in the 1996 Anglo-Italian Cup Final defeat to Genoa.

The defender spent July 1999 to January 2001 in the Third Division with Darlington and then spent the second half of the 2000/01 season at Hartlepool United. He played in play-off final defeats with Leeds, Port Vale and Darlington.

Aspin played non-league football at Harrogate Town until retiring as a player in 2004, and then managed the club from January 2005 to April 2009. He was appointed as manager of FC Halifax Town in April 2009, leading the Shaymen to three successive promotions in his first four seasons, taking them from the second tier of the Northern Premier League to the Conference Premier by winning the Northern Premier League Division One North and Premier Division titles in 2009/10 and 2010/11 and then the Conference North Play-offs in 2013; he also won the Peter Swales Shield in 2011 and the West Riding County Cup in 2013, as well as numerous manager of the month awards. However he was sacked in September 2015 after a series of poor results and two months later took charge at Gateshead. He spent two years there, before he was installed as Port Vale manager in October 2017. Neil steered the club away from relegation at the end of the 2017/18 season before tendering his resignation in January 2019.

My Memorable Match Involving Neil Aspin
Hartlepool United v Darlington – 1999/2000

I went to this game with Ian in his car. We stopped off at the Owton Lodge pub on the outskirts of Hartlepool at about one o'clock for a few beers. While a group of old men in the bar concentrated on their game of dominoes, not even noticing that we were there, the two of us focused our attention on getting served ourselves.

Later, a group of Darlington fans arrived. Fortunately, the Owton Lodge is a good pub and far enough away from the town centre to be trouble free on matchdays.

At quarter past two we left the pub and drove the short distance to the car park of the Stranton pub opposite the fire station. We arrived at Victoria Park at 20 to three and after we'd bought our programmes a steward opened the gate for my wheelchair to let us in.

As we rounded the corner, I saw Peter Shilton's permed head in the distance. His son Sam was playing for Hartlepool at that time and Peter must have been there to watch him play.

Once in the disabled area I saw fellow wheelchair-using Darlington supporter Terry Soley. To my dismay, the view was restricted for the two of us. To make matters worse, there was a man with learning difficulties bobbing up and down in front of me, obscuring my view. I complained politely to a steward, who took no notice and continued talking to someone else. I then said, 'That's the height of bad manners.' This sprang the aforementioned steward into action and he then promised to fetch someone in authority to address my complaints, but by the end of the game no one had turned up. Interestingly, Ian and I had paid £11 for the privilege of not being able to see the game properly. Terry had only paid £8.

During the match, the Pool fans in the Town End were singing 'Hodgy takes it up the ar**'. Fortunately for me, they were referring to the Darlington manager!

With the score at 2-0 to Hartlepool, we left before the final whistle sounded, dejected and convinced that no Darlington player would score that day, except possibly in his own net.

It was an excruciatingly awful performance from the Quakers. In my opinion, only Neil Aspin came out of the game with any credit. This was our main topic of conversation as we headed home.

* * *

Alan White – Career Details

Born in Darlington, Alan White began his career as a trainee at Middlesbrough in 1995, but his only first-team appearance came in the Anglo-Italian Cup. He joined Luton Town in September 1997 for a fee of £40,000 and made over 80 league appearances in three seasons. He had a one-month loan spell with Colchester United in late 1999 and joined the Layer Road club on a free transfer in July 2000.

White made 166 appearances for Colchester in four seasons, scoring four goals, and was voted the club's player of the year in 2003/04. He rejected their offer of a new contract and instead joined Leyton Orient in June 2004 on a two-year deal. However, he was allowed to leave nine months later and joined Boston United in March 2005 on a one-year contract.

At the end of his Boston deal in June 2006, Alan signed for Notts County on a free transfer, where he was made club captain. Nine months later, he joined Peterborough United on loan for the remainder of 2006/07 and was one of six players released by his parent club at the end of the season.

White joined his hometown club Darlington on 15 May 2007. He went on to make 85 league and cup appearances. The Quakers entered administration in February 2009 and White was told he would be free to leave at the end of the season. He subsequently rejoined Luton on a two-year contract on 8 June

2009. He played 24 games for the Hatters before being placed on the transfer list on 12 January 2010. Three days later he rejoined Darlington on loan for the rest of the season. He made 24 appearances as Darlington were relegated from the Football League, picking up just 30 points from 46 games.

On 27 August 2010, White was released by Luton. He was picked up by Conference North club Stalybridge Celtic and made his debut against Alfreton Town on 2 October 2010. Alan made only eight league and cup appearances for his new club before signing for Gateshead on a monthly contract on 18 November. He made his debut on 20 November in a 1-1 draw with Forest Green Rovers and scored his first goal for them on 14 December against Southport in the FA Trophy. On 8 February 2011, the club announced that they had released White.

He signed for Blyth Spartans on 11 February and made his debut four days later against Alfreton, scoring an own goal in a 2-1 defeat. He made 15 appearances by the end of the season and then rejoined Boston, then playing in the Conference North, on a non-contract basis. In mid-December he left, citing the distance he had to travel from his home in Darlington, and signed for another Conference North club, Harrogate Town. He helped them gain promotion to the Conference National in 2013, but left in October 2013 to rejoin Darlington – by then playing in the Northern Premier League Division One North under the name of Darlington 1883 – in search of regular football. Alan was named in the 2013/14 Northern Premier League Division One North Team of the Season, and contributed to two consecutive promotions in the next two seasons, as well as taking on some coaching duties.

In June 2016, Alan joined Spennymoor Town as player-coach. He remained with the club until October 2017, when he returned to Darlington as assistant to the newly appointed manager Tommy Wright. When Wright left at the end of the 2018/19 season, White stayed on as temporary academy manager until a permanent appointment was made in mid-July.

Alan is no longer involved in football and at the time of writing is in the police force.

My Memorable Match Involving Alan White
Rotherham United v Darlington – 2007/08

I went to this match with Ian in his car, my long term friend John Gray and Rob Marquiss.

With England playing Israel later in the day, our game was switched to a one o'clock kick off. With this in mind we set off at 9.30.

We arrived in Rotherham at 11 o'clock and Ian dropped us off at the Moulders Arms pub near the stadium before leaving us to visit a few villages in the surrounding area where some of his ancestors were born. Ian, like me, is really into family history and wanted to do some research prior to the match.

John, Rob and I ordered some food – burger and chips for me. While we were eating our meal we talked briefly about the forthcoming game. John and Rob thought a draw would be a good result. I agreed as only two seasons earlier Rotherham were in the Championship. This, together with the fact they were also unbeaten after their first four games, made a draw seem a likely result.

Before we knew it, Ian had rejoined us having found a possible link to his family which he seemed particularly pleased about. We had a couple of pints before heading to the ground. Once there, I sat with him in the disabled area.

Darlington started at a blistering pace and took the lead after ten minutes; David Stockdale threw the ball out to Pawel Abbott who played it to Julian Joachim who then returned it to Abbott to score with ease. After that the home side pushed forward at every opportunity but Stockdale and his defenders were equal to everything they threw at them. Alan White, I have to say, was immense. So, despite being under the cosh for large periods of the first half, we found ourselves 1-0 up at the break.

The second half was much the same as the first with Darlington having to soak up loads of pressure. However, the longer the game went on, the more confident I was that we'd win. That confidence was justified when in the 70th minute Dave Penney's men doubled their lead. Joachim was again the provider when he crossed from the right for substitute Gregg Blundell, on for Abbott, to head home into the roof of the net. It was great play by both players involved. After that, the Millers became bereft of ideas and their heads dropped and it was the Quakers who took over the ascendancy, almost scoring a third when Rob Purdie – playing on the wing that day – fired just over from around 20 yards in the 80th minute. After that the hosts were never going to score, never mind win, and this was the case at full time.

I have to say that it was an excellent performance by Darlington. Their defence was superbly marshalled by Alan White, as mentioned above, and never really looked like conceding a goal. Pawel Abbott and Tommy Wright looked a class above League Two level and both looked like scoring almost every time they got the ball in the opposition penalty area. With all this in mind, I left the ground a very contented man; my team were back at the top of the league, what more could I ask for?

On our journey home, I thought again how good Alan White had been. We were certainly lucky to have him at the club. This was my final thought before I drifted off to sleep.

* * *

Craig Liddle – Career Details

Craig Liddle began his professional career at Aston Villa in 1990. He had been a trainee prior to signing his first professional contract. However, the defender was released after just one season. Craig then made the decision to join local team Blyth Spartans, where he spent the next three seasons.

In 1994, he signed for First Division club Middlesbrough, under the management of Bryan Robson.

Four years later, 'Lidds' joined Darlington on loan in February 1998. In 16 games he made a huge impression, playing not only in defence, but also as a midfielder. On 1 July 1998 he signed for the club on a permanent basis. During his time with the Quakers, Craig showed his professional skills on the pitch and was a hugely popular club captain. Rated by fans as one of the best defenders in the Third Division, he attracted interest from other clubs. He was voted Darlington's all-time cult hero by BBC *Football Focus* viewers with 70 per cent of the ballot. His last seasons at the club were marked by injury, as his career took its toll on his body.

His 300th appearance for the Quakers, on 1 May 2004, was marked by a commemorative beer brewed by the Darwen Brewery – 'Liddle's Best' – as well as specially printed T-shirts which went on sale. On the announcement of his retirement in May 2005 Liddle was granted a testimonial against Middlesbrough in July of that year. Unfortunately, due to a hoax bomb threat the game had to be abandoned at half-time.

Liddle worked as a football coach at Darlington College from September 2005 until June 2007. In February 2008, he returned to Darlington as a youth team coach under first team manager Neil Maddison, after previous manager Mick Tait left the club. On 8 May 2009, Liddle and Maddison became joint caretaker managers, after Brackenbury Clark and Company, the administrators of the club, had released the majority of the first-team squad and the coaching and administrative staff from their contracts with immediate effect in order to save money.

With the appointment of Colin Todd as the new manager on 20 May, Liddle remained at the club as the head of youth. Todd departed on 26 September and Liddle took over as caretaker manager the following day, assisted by Maddison once again, until a replacement for Todd could be found. He ruled himself out of taking the permanent management role, saying he did not have the experience needed to run a club.

On 5 October, it was announced that the former Republic of Ireland national team manager, Steve Staunton, had been appointed as the new permanent Darlington boss. In addition to Staunton, the club brought in former Sunderland coach Kevin

Richardson as his assistant. The pair did not start their roles until later that week, while Liddle finished his stint as caretaker manager after the Football League Trophy tie against Leeds United on 6 October. On 21 March 2010, he joined Maddison as caretaker once again, following the dismissal of a hugely disappointing Staunton before Simon Davey was appointed manager on 1 April.

Craig then started a fourth spell as caretaker manager on 25 October 2011, following the dismissal of Mark Cooper. Darlington suffered financial difficulties during Liddle's spell, and his contract was terminated on 16 January 2012, along with his playing squad. After a last-minute offer of funding to the club's administrators, the team's players were reinstated; Liddle re-registered as a player, taking his previous number four shirt. However, he did not make an appearance, with the club relegated and then liquidated at the end of season.

Liddle had a spell at Sunderland as a youth team coach before being appointed as an under-18 coach at Middlesbrough. He was promoted to academy manager in January 2017. Following the departure of Garry Monk on 23 December 2017, he was appointed caretaker manager, dealing with the first-team affairs until a replacement was found. Tony Pulis was then appointed on 26 December 2017. However Craig acted as caretaker manager for that day, due to Pulis not having trained the players, and led the team to a 2-0 victory over Bolton Wanderers at the Riverside Stadium, before resuming his previous role.

Interestingly, Craig's son Ben is a semi-professional footballer who came through the academy at Middlesbrough and currently plays for Darlington at the time of writing.

My Memories of Craig Liddle

As with Kevan Smith and a few other former players throughout this book, my memories of Lidds aren't match-related.

I've known Craig since he signed for the club, and even now we keep in fairly regular contact.

As the reader may know, I'm a filmmaker and Craig kindly contributed towards *Give Them Wings* in 2019; in addition, like many other ex-Darlington players, he bought my books. I think that he has all four!

I used to enjoy meeting up with him to watch Darlington's youth team; he always had time for me, which was great.

When he was caretaker manager in 2011/12, we spoke regularly and I really got an insight into the fact that he was working with both hands tied behind his back with the football club being in administration. Although it was an extremely difficult time for all concerned, he still remained in contact with me and was extremely grateful for the financial assistance our film company, and the supporters' trust, of which I was chair at the time, gave. He personally rang me to say thank you, which shows what a gentleman he is.

Our football-related chats are always interesting and are something I look forward to, even after all these years.

I can honestly say that I'm proud to have known Craig for 25 years; he is honestly one of football's good guys!

* * *

Dan Burn – Career Details

Born in Blyth, Northumberland, Dan Burn grew up supporting Newcastle United and idolised Alan Shearer. Released by Newcastle at the age of 11, Dan played youth football for local teams New Hartley, Blyth Town and Blyth Spartans. At 16 he began working for supermarket chain Asda, when a scout from Darlington saw him playing for Blyth Spartans and he signed on professional terms on 1 July 2009.

Due to the club's financial problems and lack of available players, Burn was promoted to the first team for the first time and was an unused substitute for a 3-1 loss against Hereford United on 31 October. He then made his away league debut as a 19th-minute substitute for injured defender Mark Bower against Torquay United on 12 December, which resulted in a 5-0 loss. He then made his first start in another encounter against Torquay on 6 March 2010, which Darlington lost 3-1. He made four appearances in the 2009/10 season as Darlington were relegated to the Conference.

After this, Burn returned to the academy to further his development before being recalled to the first team by manager Mark Cooper, where he made his first appearance of the 2010/11 season in a 3-1 win against Barrow on 3 January 2011. He went on to make 15 appearances that campaign and his performances were praised by Cooper. Dan finished second behind Jamie Chandler for the club's young player of the year award.

Burn attracted interest from Premier League clubs. In order to protect their interests, Darlington gave him a two-and-a-half-year contract on improved terms.

However, on 14 April 2011, a deal was agreed for Dan to join Premier League club Fulham at the end of the season for a fee thought to be around £350,000. After signing for the London club, the central defender was sent to Fulham's reserve team to develop and learn under Billy McKinlay.

On 25 September 2012, Burn joined the then League One club Yeovil Town on a youth loan deal for an initial month. Four days later, he made his debut against Preston North End. Burn scored an own goal but then went on to score his first senior goal a minute later, although Yeovil lost 3-2. Dan managed to establish himself in the first team at Yeovil and had his loan extended twice, initially for an extra month and then for the remainder of the season. Burn then scored his second goal for Yeovil, on 2 February, in a 3-0 win over Brentford. Having previously been suspended after being booked five times during the season, Dan received a red card after a second bookable offence in a 2-0 win over Stevenage on 13 April and missed the last three matches.

After serving the three-match ban, Burn returned to the first team, playing in the first leg of the play-off semi-final, a 1-0 loss against Sheffield United. Dan then helped the club overcome the deficit in the second leg, in a 2-1 win, and he scored at Wembley for Yeovil in the play-off final to help the club win promotion to the Championship for the first time in their history. He returned to Fulham having made 41 appearances for Yeovil and scored three goals.

Ahead of the 2013/14 season, Dan stated he was keen on returning to Yeovil. However, on 3 July 2013, he signed a new contract with Fulham, keeping him at the club until at least 2015, while also moving on a season-long loan to Championship side Birmingham City. He made his debut in a 1-0 defeat at home to Watford on 3 August and remained a regular member of the starting 11. His first goal for the club was a header from a Paul Caddis cross which opened the scoring in the League Cup third round tie on 25 September, as Birmingham beat holders Swansea City 3-1.

Burn was recalled by Fulham on 2 January 2014. Afterwards, he made his first-team debut for the Cottagers on 4 January in the FA Cup third round against Norwich City at Carrow Road. Following that game, Fulham manager René Meulensteen said that he expected Burn would rejoin Birmingham on loan for the second time, but the move never happened.

He then went on to make his Premier League debut in a 2-0 loss against Arsenal on 18 January 2014. After the match, Burn's performance was praised by Meulensteen. The player was given a handful of first-team appearances until he suffered a muscle injury, After being sidelined for weeks, Burn returned to the first team on 3 May, playing 58 minutes in a 4-1 loss against Stoke City, which relegated the club to the Championship.

Dan made his first appearance of the 2014/15 season in a 1-1 draw against Cardiff City on 30 August 2014. He scored his first goal for Fulham in a League Cup tie against Doncaster Rovers on 23 September. On 21 October, he captained Fulham for the first time and scored his first league goal of the season, in a 3-3 draw against Rotherham United. However, he struggled to regain his first-team place and he spent most of the season on the substitutes' bench. On 27 January 2015 he signed a contract extension with the club, keeping him until 2016. Dan made 22 appearances and scored once in all competitions across 2014/15.

The following season, Burn provided the assist for Cauley Woodrow to equalise in the last minute of a 1-1 draw against Huddersfield Town on 22 August 2015. He was later named the man of the match by fans in a 0-0 draw against Middlesbrough on 17 October 2015. He formed a partnership with Richard Stearman and the pair helped to keep a clean sheet. Burn was named man of the match ahead of his fellow central defender. Unfortunately, he lost his first-team place under the interim management of Peter Grant, but soon regained it under the management of Stuart Gray and Slaviša Jokanović. Having become a first-team regular under Jokanović, the club had started contract talks with him. He helped Fulham retain their Championship status for the following season after they finished in 20th place and made 35 appearances in all competitions.

At the end of the 2015/16 season, Burn was surprisingly released by Fulham after his contract came to an end, and he signed a three-year contract with newly promoted Championship club Wigan Athletic.

Burn made his Wigan debut in the opening game of the season, starting in a 2-1 loss against Bristol City. After a slow start to the season, he became one of the standout performers in the team and was recognised in winning the club's player of the year award. He scored his first goal for Wigan in a 1-0 win at former club Birmingham on 7 March 2017.

Dan signed a four-year contract with Premier League club Brighton & Hove Albion on 9 August 2018 for an undisclosed fee. He was loaned back to Wigan until January 2019.

He returned to Brighton following his loan spell and made his debut on 26 January in the FA Cup third round tie against West Bromwich Albion; it finished goalless and Burn was named man of the match. He made two more starts, both in the FA Cup, and finally made his league debut for Brighton on the opening day of the 2019/20 season away to Watford, playing in a back three alongside Lewis Dunk and Shane Duffy. He continued as a fixture in the starting 11, and by the end of the year he was the only Brighton player to play every minute of their Premier League campaign. On 1 January 2020, he fractured his collarbone in a collision with Chelsea's Reece James. The injury required surgery and despite this, he was able to return to action on 8 February.

On 2 January 2021, Dan scored an own goal, gave away a penalty and picked up a yellow card in a match where Brighton came from 3-1 behind to claim a vital point in a 3-3 home draw against Wolverhampton Wanderers. He also played in Brighton's 1-0 away victory over defending champions Liverpool on 3 February, claiming their first league win at Anfield since 1982. On 18 May 2021, with fans returning to football after the COVID-19 pandemic, Burn scored his first goal for Brighton in a 3-2 home win over champions Manchester City, scoring the winner to seal the Seagulls' first top-flight victory over City since 1981.

In the absence of Lewis Dunk, Shane Duffy, Pascal Groß and several others, Dan captained the team for the first time in the 1-0 home loss to Wolves on 15 December 2021. His second Albion goal, a back-post header away to Everton on 2 January 2022, doubled their lead in a match that they won 3-2.

On 28 January 2022, Brighton rejected a £7m bid for Burn from Newcastle, the club he supported and played for as a youngster. Two days later, a fee of £13m was agreed and Dan signed a two-and-a-half-year contract with the Geordies on 31 January. The fee was officially undisclosed. He made his debut on 13 February, partnering Fabian Schär at centre-back in a 1-0 victory at home to Aston Villa, and was named as Sky Sports' man of the match.

Dan is still with Newcastle United at the time of writing.

My Memorable Match Involving Dan Burn
Darlington v Eastbourne – 2010/11

I went to this game at the Northern Echo Arena with Ian. After visiting a few pubs around Darlington town centre, the pair of us hailed a taxi and headed to the stadium, where we had booked into hospitality.

Within 40 minutes of getting into the taxi, we were tucking into our carvery. Interestingly, on our table was my friend and former club captain Kevan Smith, who I've already talked about in this book. He thought Darlington would win easily against one of the weakest teams in the Conference, by this time known as the Blue Square Bet Premier. I reminded him of the fact that we had only drawn 1-1 with them earlier in the season. Kevan, however, was adamant that the Quakers would win.

After saying our goodbyes to Kevan, Ian and I headed to our place in the disabled area, where we witnessed a brilliant Darlington performance.

The game against the bottom club was all over before half-time, when we led 5-0. Marc Bridge-Wilkinson scored direct from a free kick to open the scoring and then he quickly added two penalties. Liam Hatch headed the fourth from a Paul Arnison cross, and Paul Campbell got the fifth from the edge of the box.

In the second half, Aman Verma scored the sixth from a Bridge-Wilkinson pass, while Eastbourne scored a late consolation goal.

As my friend and I left the stadium, we both commented on how mature Dan Burn looked at the centre of Darlington's defence. Ian said, 'That lad is destined for big things.' Little did I know at that time how right he would be! I always remember this match when I look back at Dan's time at Darlington because of Ian's comment.

* * *

Terry Galbraith – Career Details

Terry joined Darlington in November 2012 from Dunston UTS where he was part of their 2011/12 FA Vase-winning side.

Capable of playing left-back, left wing and midfield, he scored one of the most important goals in Darlington's recent history when he notched the equaliser in the top-of-the-table clash at Spennymoor in January 2013. The Quakers went on to win the game 3-1 and take control at the top of the Northern League table and win the title. He ended up winning three promotion medals with Darlington, having added the Northern Premier League Division One North play-offs and NPL Premier Division championships to his collection.

The popular Galbraith left Darlington in 2020 having made 303 appearances and scored 56 goals for the club. Not bad for a defender!

Terry signed for Hebburn shortly after leaving the Quakers.

My Memorable Match Involving Terry Galbraith
Darlington v West Auckland – 2012/13

I travelled to this match at Heritage Park with Ian in his car.

On arrival at the ground, we went to the bar, had a couple of pints (more like I did – Ian only had one because he was driving), before taking our places to watch was an eventful game to say the least.

We witnessed West Auckland's Mark Stephenson get dismissed in the opening 30 minutes for two bookable offences, either side of a brilliant Terry Galbraith goal from a free kick. To compound matters, West Auckland boss Peter Dixon was shown a red card at half-time for dissent.

During the interval, my friend and I returned to the bar, our main topic of conversation was firstly Galbraith's free kick which separated the two sides and how ill-disciplined West Auckland were. Little did the pair of us know what was to follow!

In the second half, the Quakers missed a string of chances, Stephen Thompson being the main culprit, before Galbraith smashed in the second from long range on 77 minutes. The goal sparked off huge West Auckland protests, and they had former Darlington striker John Campbell sent off for dissent, while Shaun Vipond, who had been subbed, was shown his second yellow card by the overworked referee. Darlington simply played out the final 13 minutes safely in the knowledge that the victory was in the bag.

On our journey home, I said to Ian that in 40 years of watching football, I'd never seen such an unprofessional rabble as I had seen with West Auckland that day. From a football point of view, Terry Galbraith was brilliant, both in defence and attack, and was man of the match by a country mile.

* * *

Kevin Burgess – Career Details

Kevin Burgess was born in Middlesbrough and began his football career as a youngster with his hometown club. He joined Darlington in January 2007 and, after impressing in the reserves, he made his debut on the final day of the season as a second half substitute in a 5-0 defeat at home to Stockport County.

His contract was extended for another season and he was given a squad number but his only first-team appearance was as a substitute in the FA Cup and he spent the last few weeks of the season on loan to Northern Premier League Premier Division club Whitby Town. On his release from Darlington, he was promptly signed up by the seaside club for the 2008/09 season.

Kevin rejoined Darlington from Whitby prior to the 2015/16 season and was appointed captain when fellow central defender Gary Brown joined Shildon. He retained the captaincy when Brown returned early in the season and they formed a strong defensive partnership together which helped Darlington become Northern Premier League Premier Division champions, thus earning promotion to National League North.

The popular defender was made available for transfer in September 2017 and returned to Whitby in December of that year on a month's loan.

The Quakers cancelled Kevin's contract in June 2018 and he signed for Scarborough Athletic, who at that time were in the Northern Premier League Premier Division.

In June 2019, the defender joined Marske United, where he remains at the time of writing.

My Memorable Match Involving Kevin Burgess
Darlington v Rushall Olympic – 2015/16

Despite still recovering from my serious car crash and not feeling great, I decided at the last minute to go to this match with Ian.

I have to say Rushall gave Darlington their toughest game of the season and they proved really hard to break down. In their first real attack, the Quakers were awarded a free kick about 20 yards out for a foul on striker Graeme Armstrong. Full-back Terry Galbraith drove the ball goalwards and it was blocked by a visiting defender, with the home team claiming handball. In Darlington's next attack, which was started by a long throw by defender Chris Hunter, the ball was flicked towards goal by striker Liam Hardy, but the visiting keeper Kieran Preston saved. Rushall had a chance on 12 minutes when Josh Mckenzie burst down the right, got into the box and fired into the side netting. They had another opportunity eight minutes later with a 25-yarder from Alex Reid from the left that Peter Jameson held on to at the second attempt. The visitors had yet another good chance on 24 minutes when they broke away with a three on two and the ball again fell for Reid who forced Jameson to go full length and save.

Darlington had a chance on 28 minutes when Kevin Burgess headed goalwards from Galbraith's corner, but unfortunately the ball hit striker Nathan Cartman on the six-yard line. A minute later, there was a big scramble in the Rushall box, which ended after Gary Brown turned six yards out and beat the keeper with a powerful shot that struck the crossbar and was headed clear. This proved to be the last real action of the first half.

With not feeling great, Ian was both surprised and indeed amused when I turned down a pint and asked for a bottle of water once we reached the bar.

Our main topic of conversation during the interval – apart from me not having a pint – was how impressed we were with Rushall.

The second half was only six minutes old when the Quakers went close to scoring. Winger Andrew Mitchell's corner was cleared as far as midfielder Leon Scott, whose shot was deflected just wide by a defender. They finally broke the deadlock on 53 minutes. A cross by Mitchell from the right went over to the far post where Brown played the ball back at full stretch for Burgess to score from six yards, his eighth league goal of the season. Ian and I were mightily relieved as we both thought that it was going to be one of those days. Rushall missed a good chance to level on 61 minutes. Reid got to the byline and pulled the ball back into the middle where Jake Heath, coming in at the far post, side-footed just over the top. Three minutes later, there was a real mix-up in the Rushall defence when Preston collided with a defender while going for the ball which fell for Thompson, who blasted his shot wide. Striker Lee Gaskell nearly scored Darlington's second on 79 minutes. He picked the ball up on the left, neatly beat a defender, and chipped just past the far post. The same player missed another opportunity four minutes later, but his attempted back-heel was blocked by a visiting defender. This was the last real chance either side had.

As I sat watching television later that evening, I reflected to myself that it had been a close game, but Kevin Burgess had certainly been the difference between the two teams. This wasn't only because he scored the winning goal; he was also composed in defence and was certainly my man of the match that day.

* * *

David Ferguson – Career Details

Sunderland-born David Ferguson began his career in Darlington's youth system, breaking into the first team in early 2012. He finished the 2011/12 season with six Blue Square Bet Premier League appearances.

Ferguson signed for Premier League club Sunderland in June 2012 on a one-year contract. He went out on loan to Boston United in Blue Square Bet North and made his debut on 1 March 2014 when he started in a 4-0 home win over Hednesford Town.

David joined Championship club Blackpool on 9 January 2015 on a one-and-a-half-year contract, with the option of a further year. He scored his first professional goal on 14 February 2015 in a 4-4 home draw with Nottingham Forest, in only his second appearance. The goal was a header from a Jamie O'Hara cross in the seventh minute of stoppage time, and earned his side a point. On 4 August 2015, the full-back was appointed as team captain. Unfortunately, he was released at the end of the 2015/16 season.

He signed for Northern League Division One club Shildon in August 2016 but moved back to Darlington, now in National League North, the following January. Ferguson played for England C for the first time in May 2017.

On 6 October 2017, David signed for Darlington's National League North rivals York City on a contract running to June 2019, after York activated a release clause in his contract. He was signed by manager Martin Gray (more of whom later), who had left Darlington for York just days earlier. He gave up a job in refuse upon returning to full-time football with the Minstermen.

Ferguson signed for National League club Hartlepool United on 5 August 2020 after turning down the offer of a new contract with York City. He scored his first goal for his new club with a free kick in a 2-0 home win against Solihull Moors. He started in the 2021 National League play-off final as Hartlepool were promoted back to the EFL. In 2020/21, David contributed 11 assists. His performances earned him a place in the 2020/21 National League Team of the Year.

In January 2022, Ferguson scored the equaliser against Blackpool – by now of the Championship – in a 2-1 win as Hartlepool reached the fourth round of the FA Cup. On 6 May 2022, David signed a new-two year contract.

My Memorable Match Involving David Ferguson
Darlington v FC United of Manchester – 2016/17

I went with Ian and the two of us witnessed a very good Darlington performance.

We saw Darlington have the first chance when striker Stephen Thompson got around his man on the right and forced a save out of visiting keeper Ryan Schofield. The Quakers scored from their next attack when the ball came to David Ferguson 25 yards out, and he hit a blistering left-footed shot that flew into the top corner past the helpless Schofield – his first goal for the club! Shortly after, FC United hit back, and keeper Adam Bartlett had to dash off his line and save at the feet of Chris Chantler. But the home side went up the other end and nearly got a second with a shot by winger Josh Gillies that Schofield saved.

It was 2-0 on 13 minutes when Ferguson crossed well from the left for David Syers to head back for Mark Beck to head his 16th league goal of the season. Bartlett had to be alert again when Kieran Glynn got through, but he blocked his shot with his outstretched hand. Darlington were awarded a penalty on 26 minutes when Beck was tripped by Jake Williams as he latched on to the ball in the area. The referee pointed to the spot from where left-back Terry Galbraith tucked away the penalty for his 12th league goal of the season. Shortly after the restart, a great flowing move involving five players ended with Gillies back-heeling for Ferguson to have a shot well saved by Schofield. In Darlington's next attack, Beck headed against the post as the hosts were threatening to run riot.

FC United eventually got back into the game and pulled a goal back on 34 minutes when Matthew Wolfenden got down the right and pulled the ball back for Tom Brown to swivel and place it into the bottom corner. It was nearly 4-1 though on 41 minutes. Defender Gary Brown threw the ball long into the area, and Beck's header towards goal landed on the roof of the net in what turned out to be the last real action of the opening period.

Ian and I were certainly happy as we headed to the bar for our half-time pint!

Darlington started the second period like an express train and had a half chance on 49 minutes when Gillies found striker

Nathan Cartman on the left and he tried to lift the ball over Schofield from the corner of the box, but unfortunately for the home fans, it drifted wide. The Quakers were once again denied by Schofield on 56 minutes. Thompson crossed from the right and Brown nodded the ball down for Cartman, whose low shot was blocked by the outstretched leg of the keeper. FC United then missed a great chance to pull another one back when Wolfenden nodded down a left-wing cross for Brown ten yards out, but he swept the ball wide. Another opportunity for the home side came along on 70 minutes when clever play by Beck allowed Cartman to send Ferguson up the left, and the full-back's first-time shot was pushed around the post by Schofield. Gary Brown went up to support his attack, and he went close with a header from a Thompson cross on 75 minutes that went just wide. However, the visitors weren't done, and their substitute Tomi Adeloye found space inside the box and hit a right-footed shot that Bartlett palmed over the bar. The hosts' fourth goal finally came when Brown controlled a cross from the right, played a one-two with Cartman, and slotted the ball home for his fifth league goal of the season.

But still FC United kept going, and Bartlett pulled off a good save low down from Wolfenden, then Adeloye headed into the bottom-left corner for 4-2 and that was the last of the scoring.

As Ian pushed me back to his car, we both agreed that David Ferguson had been excellent during the whole match and was an excellent signing by Martin Gray. Ian added, 'We'd be lucky to keep hold of him if he continued to play like that.' Once again, he was right, as a few months later he followed Gray to York City, as mentioned above.

* * *

Gary Brown – Career Details
Gary Brown had two spells at Darlington. He was originally signed by Martin Gray after just one training session ahead of the Northern League season in the summer of 2012 and was

immediately made club captain; it turned out to be a really good move for the player.

He is recognised as a central defender, but he can also play at full-back and in midfield if needed. He joined Darlington after playing for Durham City, Jarrow Roofing and Blyth Spartans in their 2008/09 Conference North days where he was involved in their memorable FA Cup run which saw them reach the third round.

Gary suffered a knee injury in the summer of 2013 and he missed the first five months of the season, but he returned as strong as ever.

He led the Quakers to victory in the NPL Division One North play-offs in 2014/15, and actually played in goal at Lancaster City along the way.

For family reasons he joined Northern League club Shildon during the summer of 2015, but decided to return to the club four months later, and formed a very strong partnership in the heart of their defence with Kevin Burgess – the 'B and B' partnership that helped the Quakers to win the Northern Premier League title in 2016/17.

Gary had a caretaker spell in charge of the team with fellow player Phil Turnbull after Martin Gray quit the club to go to York City in October 2017, before leaving the club under Tommy Wright's reign.

My Memorable Match Involving Gary Brown
Darlington v Ilkeston Town 2016/17

Once again, I went with Ian, where we were lucky enough to see another excellent performance from our beloved Darlington.

The pair of us were barely in our places when the home side almost took the lead. Stephen Thompson won possession on the right, made good ground and crossed low into the middle where Lee Gaskell went full length to force the ball towards goal from a few yards, but somehow keeper Jamie Hannis kept it out. However, we didn't have to wait very long for the first goal to arrive as the Quakers took the lead after ten minutes.

Thompson curled a corner over from the left; the ball went all the way over to the far post for Nathan Cartman to turn home his 12th league goal of the season.

It was almost 2-0 on 14 minutes when Cartman nodded the ball down for Thompson to drive just wide and he got another shooting chance just after the quarter-hour mark, but once again Hannis saved. Another opportunity came along on 17 minutes when defender Chris Hunter's free kick fell for Gary Brown, who volleyed just wide; two minutes later, Thompson sent Cartman through, and from about 30 yards he lobbed Hannis, but a defender got back and cleared.

The second goal duly arrived on 22 minutes. Brown's long throw was helped on at the near post, and Gaskell headed in from a few yards, his 14th league goal of the season. Darlington went 3-0 up on 33 minutes as Terry Galbraith's corner to the far post was headed back by Burgess for Brown to head in from point-blank range. At that point I said to Ian, 'Game over.' My friend smiled knowingly. Shortly after my comment, Gaskell went for the fourth goal when he picked up the ball in the inside-left position and made good ground, but he fired wide from the edge of the box.

As was the norm that season, Ian and I were two happy chappies as we headed to the bar for our customary half-time pint.

At the start of the second half, a concerted spell of pressure ended with midfielder Phil Turnbull firing just wide from 30 yards. The same player went even closer on 54 minutes, when fellow midfielder Leon Scott played the ball back perfectly for him to hit low and hard; unfortunately, the ball missed the target by a whisker. The hosts suddenly moved up a gear and almost scored a fourth when Liam Hardy picked up a crossfield pass, sidestepped a defender and hit a right-footed shot that Hannis just managed to tip over the bar. Credit to the visitors, they kept battling away and Danny Udoh pulled a goal back for them in the last minute to make the final score 3-1.

As we headed back to the car, we both agreed that Gary

Brown had been immense in the game, contributing a part assist with his long throw and also a goal. I said to my friend as he put me in the car that Gary reminded me of Kevan Smith because of his leadership skills. I honestly can't praise a player any higher than that!

3

Midfielders and Wingers

Barry Lyons – Career Details

Born in Shirebrook, Derbyshire, Barry Lyons started his career with Rotherham United in 1963, making his debut in September of that year. He moved to Nottingham Forest for £45,000 in November 1966. During the time he was at the club, he came close to earning a cap for the England under-23 team. He was a part of the team that finished runners-up in the First Division in 1966/67.

Barry joined York City for £12,000 in September 1973, where showed some classy performances as the Minstermen clinched promotion. He scored their first goal in the higher division, which came against Aston Villa. He moved to Darlington on a free transfer in April 1976 and finished his playing career with the club.

Lyons returned to York City as youth team coach in 1979. He became caretaker manager in March 1980 as they were battling to avoid re-election, which they succeeded in doing and he was given the job permanently. He was however removed from the role in December 1981 due to poor results, with York having had to seek re-election at the end of the 1980/81 season. He continued in the role of youth team manager until July 1982.

My Memorable Match Involving Barry Lyons

Darlington v Fulham, League Cup second round replay – 1978/79

Not for the first time, I skived off school to go to this midweek game with my mother. Thinking about it, not many mothers would let their child stay off school to attend a football match. I was very lucky that mine did, more than once!

Having drawn 2-2 at Craven Cottage, with Derek Craig and Dennis Wann scoring our goals, I can remember entering my beloved Feethams in the pouring rain eagerly anticipating the replay against the Second Division side.

As my mother and I sat in the East Stand Paddock watching the match against a team who were two leagues above us, I can remember thinking that the rain was proving to be a leveller and it came as no surprise to me when the score was 0-0 at the interval.

However, that changed in the 63rd minute when Barry Lyons, the former Nottingham Forest star, scored the only goal of the game from the penalty spot after Terry Bullivant and Kevin Lock combined to bring down our speedy right-winger Lloyd Maitland to earn his team a plum third round tie away at First Division Everton.

I can remember being overjoyed as my mother and I ventured home in the still pouring rain. All I could talk about was the way Barry Lyons blasted the penalty into the visitors' net!

* * *

Lloyd Maitland – Career Details

Lloyd Maitland was born in Coleshill, Warwickshire, and played for Huddersfield Town from 1974 to 1977 and then Darlington between 1977 and 1979.

He was a fast, tricky right-winger and was the first black player to play for Huddersfield's first team, in 1975. Lloyd also played in Town's FA Youth Cup Final team versus Tottenham Hotspur in 1974.

Lloyd retired from football in 1979, after being run over by a car driven by then Darlington team-mate Eric Probert.

My Memories of Lloyd Maitland

My first memory of Lloyd was when I used to go to Feethams with my mother. I was amazed by the skills he had and despite all the racial abuse he got, it never seemed to bother him. Even as a child I admired him for that. In many ways it reminded me of the situation I was in and the discrimination I faced in the 1970s and 1980s. Every time things happened to me, for example not getting in a pub or football ground because I was in a wheelchair, I thought of the abuse Lloyd – even long after he'd left Darlington – took simply because of his colour, which wasn't right then and it certainly isn't now. It spurred me on and even now, I'm eternally grateful to him for that.

I can remember the day Lloyd was run over by Eric Probert and later having to retire from the game because of his injuries. The Quakers lost a really talented player, one who helped me more than he'll ever know.

* * *

David McLean – Career Details

David McLean started his career with hometown club Newcastle United but found opportunities limited. He moved on to Carlisle United but established himself as a regular when he signed for Darlington in 1979.

The hard-working midfielder enjoyed a successful seven-year stay with the Quakers, becoming a key player in the process. He helped Darlington win promotion under Cyril Knowles in 1985. David moved on to Scunthorpe United in 1986, and later joined Whitley Bay. Interestingly in 2003, David was voted as part of Darlington's all-time XI to coincide with the club's departure from Feethams.

My Memorable Match Involving David McLean

Darlington v Rochdale – 1980/81

Once again I skived off school and went to this match with my mother. I have to say, this was an excellent decision, as the two of us watched an enthralling game of football.

The Quakers saw the visitors make a determined start and completely dominate the opening exchanges. Prompted by ex-Darlington winger Dennis Wann, keen to impress against his old club, Rochdale forced seven corners in the first 15 minutes and regularly tore huge holes in Darlington's fragile defence, who were probably distracted by the garish red-and-green-striped kit that the visitors turned out in. Rochdale found themselves two goals up after ten minutes through Brian Taylor and Dave Esser and it looked like it was going to be a long night for the Feethams faithful. The hosts fought back though, and pulled a goal back midway through the half when David Speedie was tripped in the box by Wann and David McLean stroked home the penalty. This made it a much more even contest and they equalised just before the break when Alan Walsh fired in a powerful long-range shot that was parried by visiting keeper Graeme Crawford. Speedie was the first to react and slotted home the rebound for his first goal for the club.

Darlington began the second half on top and the turnaround was complete when they scored a third goal on 48 minutes. A Harry Charlton corner was scrambled clear by the Rochdale defence but unfortunately for them the ball fell perfectly for Walsh, who smashed a 25-yarder through the crowded goalmouth and into the net with Crawford helpless. The entertainment continued and the visitors drew level with a spectacular free kick from right-back Alan Jones, who matched Walsh's power from 20 yards out and it was Barry Siddall's turn to look on helplessly. Within a minute Darlington were back in front after a clumsy tackle by Peter Burke brought down McLean in the box and he picked himself up to confidently convert his second penalty of the evening. The Quakers couldn't hold on though and Rochdale escaped with a point when they equalised again with virtually the last kick of the game. A corner led to a crazy goalmouth scramble which ended with Barry Wellings forcing the ball over the line from close range.

As I lay in bed later in the evening, I couldn't help but think how good David McLean was in that match. Not only because he scored two goals; also because in my opinion, he, Alan Walsh and David Speedie were the best three players on the park by a country mile.

* * *

Ian Hamilton – Career Details

Ian Hamilton was born in South Shields. He began his professional football career with the then Fourth Division club Darlington, joining from Boldon Colliery Welfare in 1979.

Over three seasons, Ian scored 19 goals in 103 appearances in league matches for the Quakers, and in 1982 he moved to Belgium where he settled.

He spent a season in the second tier with La Louvière before moving up to the top flight with Liège. In his second season with Liège, Hamilton helped the club qualify for the UEFA Cup, but made what he later described as the greatest mistake of his career by walking out because they refused him a pay rise. Ian returned to La Louvière, where he spent five years playing in the third tier. He dropped down another division with Binche, a club he later managed.

My Memorable Match Involving Ian Hamilton
Darlington v Mansfield Town – 1980/81

My mother and I were lucky enough to be in the ground on the day that Darlington became the first club in the country to officially stage a Sunday fixture in the Football League when they played Mansfield Town at Feethams in February 1981.

With national television and press coverage focused on the game our average gate of 2,500 had swelled to an impressive 5,932. According to local reporter Mike Amos in the *Northern Echo*, the club had arranged for 2,000 programmes to be printed and had purchased 1,000 pies, all of which were sold!

After Ian Hamilton converted a penalty, Mansfield scored twice and we needed a rare headed goal in the 88th minute from regular scorer Alan Walsh to earn Darlington a creditable 2-2 draw.

As my mother pushed me home, I thought that Ian Hamilton had been excellent in midfield for the Quakers and had put in a solid, hard-working performance. This was capped with him going into the record books for scoring the first goal in the first official Sunday Football League match. This was long before the introduction of Sky Sports. I suppose that in some ways, he could be described as a trailblazer for what was to come!

* * *

Roger Wicks – Career Details

Roger Wicks was born in Warrington and made 41 Football League appearances as a midfielder for Darlington in the early 1980s.

He also played non-league football for clubs including Netherfield and Newcastle Blue Star.

Roger also had a spell as manager of the then Northern League Division Two club Darlington Cleveland Bridge in the early 1990s.

At the time of writing, Roger works in a hospital for adults with autism.

My Memories of Roger Wicks

I've known Roger since 1980 – let me explain.

He married a girl called Valerie who lived in my street when I was growing up and that's how I first met him; I was still at school then.

Eventually he and Valerie got their own place but we kept in touch and over the years he, like many other former players, has supported me in whatever I have done. For example, he has played in many charity football matches that I've organised over the years and he even put some money into our film (as did dozens of other former players and I have to say, that I'm extremely grateful to each and every one of them), *Give Them Wings*, which came out to great acclaim in July 2022. I'm pleased to say that Roger and I are still in regular contact to this day and I regard him as a friend. Every time I hold an event, Roger is always one of the first people on my list to invite.

One day I hope to collaborate with him on a script, as he is now a writer, as well as being a support worker in a hospital for adults with autism, as mentioned above.

* * *

David Hawker – Career Details

David Hawker made 130 appearances in the Football League for Hull City and Darlington in the 1970s and 1980s. A midfielder, he also played non-league football for several clubs including Bishop Auckland, Brandon United and Whitley Bay, for whom he scored as Bay won the 1986/87 Northumberland Senior Cup Final, and South Bank.

Interestingly David played for Darlington on three separate occasions: 1980/82, 1982/83 and 1984/85.

My Memorable Match Involving David Hawker

Crewe Alexandra v Darlington – 1982/83

I went to this match with John Gray on the supporters' club coach.

On arrival at the ground we learned that Dave Hawker had been re-signed on a short-term contract, following his release the previous season, and was on the bench. I'd always liked David and was disappointed when he'd been let go.

The pair of us saw Darlington turn in a complete performance and dominate the game from start to finish. They took the lead in the 19th minute when a fierce Alan Walsh drive was blocked by home goalkeeper Steve Smith. The ball rebounded to the edge of the box where it was met by Tim Gilbert who drove it home. The Quakers continued to drive forward and had two strong claims for penalties turned down. Barry Dunn was brought down by home defender Neil Salathiel when in full flight, shortly after his shot had appeared to be fisted away by central defender Bob Scott. Crewe were hanging on but conceded a second goal five minutes before half-time.

Harry Wilson played the ball to the edge of the Crewe area to Tony McFadden who superbly nodded it back into the path of Dave McLean. His fierce drive from 20 yards out flew into the roof of the net. The half ended with an injury concern for the impressive Gilbert who went down after a clash of heads with Bernard Purdie.

Unfortunately, the shaken and concussed Gilbert was unable to continue and was replaced at half-time by Dave Hawker. The change didn't seem to disrupt the visitors much. They still played all the flowing football and threatened more goals every time they attacked. Their third goal came after 56 minutes when Walsh cracked a shot against the foot of the post and Dunn coolly picked his spot and swept the rebound home. In a rare home attack Crewe gave themselves some hope with a goal of their own on 62 minutes. A Clive Evans shot came back off the woodwork and Steve Craven reacted quicker than Kevan Smith to stab the ball home.

The home team's revival never really happened though, and Darlington increased their lead in the 70th minute. A McLean corner was flicked on by Walsh and volleyed home by Smith at the far post. The waves of attacks by the visitors continued and they scored their fifth of the night in the 86th minute. A sweeping 60-yard pass from Walsh sent McFadden racing into the box. He held off Scott's challenge and drilled his shot between keeper Smith and the near post. There was still time for Crewe to grab a second consolation goal on 88 minutes, when Evans headed home a Dave Goodwin cross after a defensive mix-up.

John and I were certainly happy as we headed home on the coach.

I can remember thinking that it had been good to see David Hawker in a Darlington shirt again and considering he hadn't had a proper pre-season, he'd done really well in the heart of the midfield in my humble opinion.

* * *

Mike Angus – Career Details

Mike Angus made 75 appearances in the Football League as a midfielder for Middlesbrough, Scunthorpe United and Darlington, whom he helped win promotion to the Third Division in season 1984/85.

He also made a single appearance for Southend United in the League Cup and later played non-league football for Guisborough Town and South Bank.

After retiring from football, Mike joined the police force.

My Memorable Match Involving Mike Angus

Middlesbrough v Darlington, FA Cup third round – 1984/85

I went to the match on the Football Special train service, again with my friend Stephen Lowson.

Once in Middlesbrough, Stephen pushed me along Linthorpe Road towards the ground, stopping off at a few pubs on the way. Although British Rail had put on buses to the ground for the Darlington fans, there was no way that I could have got on board one of those in my wheelchair.

On entering the ground, a couple of stewards gave Stephen a hand to carry me up into one of the seats in the home end. It was a bitterly cold afternoon and the pitch was covered in snow, while sleet showers drifted in from the North Sea.

As I was waiting for the game to start, I can remember thinking that this was always going to be a needle match because of the number of former Boro players in the Darlington squad. Apart from Cyril Knowles himself, there were several with Middlesbrough connections. Footballers revel in the knowledge that they might be able to put one over on their old club. Interestingly, several of the Boro players who were part of their squad at that particular time later went on to play for the Quakers, such as David Currie, Tony McAndrew, Alan Roberts and Paul Ward.

Getting to the game itself, to this day, I'm still convinced that Garry MacDonald scored a perfectly valid goal but the referee, wrongly in my opinion, adjudged that the ball hadn't crossed the line. Mick Saxby, the Boro defender, claimed to have hacked it away from the muddy goalmouth, but it was well over the line from where I was sat.

I have to say, Mike Angus was excellent in midfield; he ran his heart out against his former club in what was a very entertaining 0-0 draw.

* * *

Steve Tupling – Career Details

Steve Tupling was born in 1964 in Wensleydale, which was then in the North Riding of Yorkshire. He began his football career with Middlesbrough, but never played in the Football League for them. Following his departure, he played in the Football League for Carlisle United, Darlington (two spells), Newport County, Cardiff City, Torquay United, Exeter City (both on loan), and Hartlepool United. He also played non-league football for Gateshead following his second spell with Darlington. After retiring from full-time football, Steve became a teacher at a school in Whitley Bay.

My Memorable Match Involving Steve Tupling

Derby County v Darlington – 1985/86

I went to the Baseball Ground to see this match with Ian in another couple's car.

The game provided us with something to cheer about – the Quakers' sturdy defence of John Green and Peter Robinson somehow managed to tame the potent Derby strike force of Bobby Davison and Trevor Christie, although the latter did score after 25 minutes. However, Green was eventually led from the field and substituted in the 59th minute after a clash of heads with Davison. A minute later Carl Airey touched on a free kick to Paul Ward who hammered it into the net to give us a creditable 1-1 draw.

Another interesting fact from that match was that Steve Tupling was bizarrely sent off in the third minute of injury time for retaliation against John Gregory – he kicked a bucket of water in his direction – who would later become manager of Aston Villa and then Derby.

Ian's and my main topic of conversation on our way home was the sending off. I'd never seen anything like it in the 14 years I'd supported Darlington. It's certainly something that I haven't forgotten to this day.

* * *

Paul Ward – Career Details

Paul began his career with Chelsea and played in the Football League for Middlesbrough, Darlington, Leyton Orient, Scunthorpe United and Lincoln City, before playing non-league football for Gainsborough Trinity.

His first experience as a manager was when he was asked to take over Darlington for the last 13 matches of their Third Division relegation season. He was at the time the youngest ever manager of a Football League club but reverted to playing duties after the end of the season. Ward also had a brief spell as manager of Harrogate Town in 1999.

In August 2002, Paul commenced a second spell as manager of Hatfield Main. He steered the club to the verge of promotion to the Premier Division of the Northern Counties East Football League before a late loss of form saw them finish in fifth place and then resign from the league due to financial problems. Ward departed to become joint manager, with Des Bennett, of Armthorpe Welfare.

In August 2013 he was appointed first team coach at Retford United, rising to the role of manager in June 2014. However, he parted company with the club. On 5 May 2015, he joined Staveley Miners Welfare as assistant to the newly appointed manager Brett Marshall. He remained in post for six and a half years until, in November 2021, Marshall and his assistants, Ward and Ian Bowling, resigned.

As of the time of writing Paul owns and runs a health and fitness club in Doncaster, which he opened following his retirement from professional football in 1994.

My Memorable Match Involving Paul Ward
Darlington v Bury – 1986/87

I witnessed Paul Ward's first home game as manager with Ian from our usual vantage point in the East Stand Paddock.

The two of us saw the Quakers tear into their visitors and grab the lead after only six minutes. David Currie found Mark Hine with a clever pass and the midfielder drilled the ball into the bottom corner from just outside the box. Six minutes later the home side were two goals up. Good work by full-back Chris Evans and winger Alan Roberts down the right resulted in a low cross by the latter that was side-footed home from close range by defender Peter Robinson. Roberts got himself on the score sheet on 27 minutes when his long-range shot was deflected by defender Nigel Hart and looped up over Bury keeper Simon Farnworth into the net. Five minutes later Roberts almost added a fourth, but his shot crashed back off the crossbar.

Prompted by Sammy McIlroy in the Bury midfield, the visitors battled to get back into the game and were given some hope on 67 minutes when substitute Liam Robinson was brought down by Paul Ward in the area. Robinson picked himself up and made no mistake from the spot. Darlington were always in control though with Currie and Stewart Ferebee combining well up front. Currie was denied three times by Farnworth in the second half before eventually having the last laugh in the final minute. He chased a long clearance by midfielder Steve Tupling, skipped past two defenders and left Farnworth floundering in the mud as he waltzed past him before slipping the ball into the unguarded net, making the final score 4-1.

As Ian pushed me back to the car, we both agreed that Paul Ward had made an excellent start to his managerial reign.

* * *

Alan Roberts – Career Details
Alan Roberts made 203 appearances in the Football League for Middlesbrough, Darlington, Sheffield United and Lincoln

City in the 1980s. He played on the right wing and had pace to burn and a direct style.

Alan was a regular in the Sheffield United side promoted from the Third Division in 1988/89, his only full season with the club, and provided numerous assists for the forward line. Transfer-listed at his own request early the following season, he joined Lincoln City in October 1989 for £60,000. He played his last match on 1 January 1990 before his career was ended at the age of 25 because of injury.

My Memorable Match Involving Alan Roberts
Port Vale v Darlington – 1986/87

I went to this game on the train with John Gray and our mutual friend Richard Jones. At the time, Ian had family in the Stoke area, so after having a few pints we met up with him outside Vale Park.

Luckily, the lads managed to get me into the away end where we witnessed an excellent Darlington performance, considering the circumstances.

The Quakers hadn't registered a single victory away from home all that season and time was running out. Andy Jones scored first for Vale in the 31st minute then Alan Roberts headed in an equaliser ten minutes later. In the second half Port Vale goalkeeper Alex Williams couldn't hold a stinging Roberts drive and Stephen Bell (now sadly no longer with us) tapped in the rebound in the 65th minute. So, when we won that day you can imagine the celebrations in the away end.

After saying our goodbyes to Ian, John, Richard and I went to Stoke where we went around a few pubs.

Our main topic of conversation was how well Darlington had played and how Alan Roberts had torn the Port Vale defence apart with his sheer pace.

I was certainly a happy man as John pushed me through my front door, well after midnight!

* * *

Paul Emson – Career Details

Paul Emson scored 38 goals in 321 appearances in the Football League for Derby County, Grimsby Town and Darlington, as a left-winger.

He began his career in the Grimsby & District League before moving into senior non-league football with Brigg Town and later played in the Conference for Kettering Town and Gateshead.

After retiring from football, Paul became a postman.

My Memorable Match Involving Paul Emson

Cheltenham Town v Darlington – 1989/90

Ian and I travelled to Cheltenham on the supporters' coach in December 1989.

History was about to be made – this was the first meeting between Darlington and Cheltenham, so it was my first visit to their ground. Having left Feethams at about eight in the morning, we stopped off at the Trowell service station near Nottingham before continuing our journey to Cheltenham, arriving there at about one o'clock in the afternoon.

When our driver pulled into a superstore car park near the Robins' Whaddon Road ground, the police ordered all the supporters to stay onboard the coach. Since I had no intention of remaining on the coach, I told a little white lie and said that I had to get off and empty my catheter bag. Just to confirm, I'm not fitted with a catheter at all, I just use a plastic bottle if I need to urinate, but the police weren't to know that. So, a kind officer let Ian get me off the coach and we went for four or five pints in two or three different pubs (in one of those pubs, we met Stephen, who later accompanied us to the match) while the remaining supporters stayed put. This was one of those very rare occasions when being disabled had its advantages!

The game itself was a scrappy affair, a situation that wasn't helped by the blustery wind and driving rain. Cheltenham had signed Andy Gray, the former Aston Villa and Scotland striker, from Glasgow Rangers during the close-season, but he limped off four minutes into the second half. In any event, his impact on the match had been very minimal – if memory serves me right, he did nothing but mouth off to the referee and moan at his team-mates!

Although Les McJannet was harshly sent off for the Quakers in the 24th minute, we still won 1-0 thanks to an 82nd-minute goal from flying winger Paul Emson. So, it was a good day all round. Interestingly, Stephen simply couldn't contain his excitement and before we could stop him he had easily jumped over the low perimeter fence as he attempted to sprint across the pitch to congratulate the scorer. But because of the heavy ground, he couldn't catch Emson, so he eventually gave up and rejoined the crowd. Fortunately, Stephen's rush of blood occurred in more enlightened times when a fan who strayed on to the pitch wasn't liable to be bundled away by stewards and banned for life.

As a matter of interest, Cheltenham Spa struck me as quite an unlikely hotbed of football. Although the team was sponsored by Gulf Oil, who had their headquarters in the town, the programme only reinforced my initial impression: the front cover photograph sported a fine row of elegant Regency houses and beautifully tended flowerbeds. More like Harrogate, in fact, than places I was used to visiting, such as Hartlepool!

Anyway, returning to the game, Paul Emson was certainly the difference between the two sides; this was Ian's and my main topic of conversation during our long journey home.

* * *

Andy Toman – Career Details

Midfielder Andy Toman started his career in the Northern League with Shildon, before joining Bishop Auckland. In the summer of 1985, he was offered his first taste of league football when Lincoln City paid £10,000 to secure his services. After a season with the Imps, Andy returned to Bishop Auckland. In January 1987, Hartlepool United offered him a second chance at league football, paying Bishop Auckland £6,000 for him.

In the summer of 1989, a £40,000 fee saw him link up with Brian Little's Darlington for their successful campaign in the Conference. He remained at Feethams for a further three seasons before joining Scarborough on loan at the end of the 1992/93 season, and being released in the summer of 1993.

He joined Scunthorpe United for the 1993/94 season but despite scoring five goals in just 15 league appearances, he moved on to join Scarborough, this time on a permanent basis. He remained with them until the summer of 1996 which marked the end of his professional career after making 317 league appearances and scoring 50 goals.

He then linked up with Whitby Town, scoring in their 3-0 FA Vase final victory over North Ferriby United at Wembley on 10 May 1997. After three seasons at the Turnbull Ground he had a short spell at Blyth Spartans, leaving after being sent off for dissent towards his own goalkeeper in a 5-3 defeat to Leigh RMI in the FA Cup on 18 September 1999. He joined Barrow where he remained until the end of that season.

On retiring from playing football, Andy had several managerial roles at Northern League clubs. As well as these, he also had a spell in Norway where he was a coach.

My Memorable Match Involving Andy Toman
Darlington v Swindon Town, League Cup first round first leg – 1990/91

I attended with Ian. As per the norm, the pair of us sat in our usual places.

The visitors started brightly and completely dominated the first 20 minutes with their fluent passing style. The Quakers were struggling to get into the game but still managed the two best chances of the half, when hitting Town on the break. In the ninth minute, Paul Emson fired in a close-range shot which was saved in spectacular fashion by Swindon's former Manchester United keeper Fraser Digby, and in the 23rd minute John Borthwick hit a fierce drive, but Digby proved his agility again with another flying save. Both chances were created by his strike partner David Cork, who also had two goals disallowed, one for pushing and one for offside. At the other end Mark Prudhoe made two good saves to keep Duncan Shearer out. The half finished goalless but ended on a sour note after a tackle from behind by Darlington's midfielder Gary Gill left Dave Bennett with a broken left leg.

Darlington began the second half on top. Digby saved shots from Borthwick and Cork with his legs, before he was finally beaten in the 50th minute. Les McJannet slipped a neat ball to Gill down the right-hand edge of the box. He had timed his run perfectly to stay onside and his square pass across the face of the goal was met by Cork, who tucked it neatly under Digby from six yards out. Swindon tried to hit back but Brian Little's men always looked capable of more goals. Andy Toman was next to try his luck but lashed a fierce volley just wide and into the side netting in the 61st minute. Twelve minutes from time, the home side got the second goal that their play deserved. Borthwick broke from his own half, evading several tackles before slipping the ball to Cork, who was upended by Ross MacLaren. Cork managed to force the ball into the net as he went down, but the referee had already awarded the penalty. Frank Gray made no mistake from the spot. Things got even better for the home side in the 86th minute when John Gittens made a complete mess of an attempted headed back-pass from a McJannet cross, leaving Cork with a simple close-range tap-in for his second of the night, to complete a resounding – if somewhat unexpected – 3-0 win.

I have to say, Andy Toman had a great game in the Darlington midfield. He literally ran himself into the ground. His pairing with Gary Gill was one of the best in the league that season.

* * *

Gary Gill – Career Details

Gary Gill began his career playing for his hometown club Middlesbrough, making his professional debut in April

1984. The club endured severe financial trouble during this period but despite this, Gill was part of the side that won consecutive promotions in 1987 and 1988 to reach the First Division before suffering a broken leg in 1989. He made just one further appearance for Boro before joining Darlington in 1989, following a loan spell with Hull City. He later played for Cardiff City, winning the Welsh Cup in 1992, before retiring at the age of 28 due to injury.

After working as a coach in the US, Gary joined Gateshead as assistant manager before taking control of the team in February 2002 following the resignation of Paul Proudlock. He resigned from the role eight months later.

Later in 2002, Gary was seriously injured after being involved in a car accident when a van hit another car before colliding with his car. He suffered a smashed left knee, a collapsed lung, a broken shoulder and a fractured neck, leaving him permanently disabled after losing full use of his left leg. The driver of the van was killed and his employer later accepted liability for the accident after it was revealed that he had been working longer hours than as permitted by law.

Gill later joined BBC Radio Cleveland, replacing his former team-mate Paul Kerr and providing match commentaries for Middlesbrough matches, and was eventually given a regular column for BBC Tees entitled 'Gilly's View'. He also worked as a buyer for a men's clothing brand and owned the Chadwick's Inn pub in Maltby.

In October 2011, Gary returned to Middlesbrough as a European scout for manager Tony Mowbray. Following Mowbray's sacking, he was moved to a new role as head of UK recruitment after the appointment of Aitor Karanka and was placed in charge of opposition scouting and the club's scouting network.

My Memorable Match Involving Gary Gill
Darlington v Carlisle United – 1990/91

I witnessed this match from my usual spot in the East Stand Paddock with my buddy Ian.

The first thing we noticed as we took our places was the state of the Feethams pitch. It was an absolute mud bath.

However, the Quakers made light of the conditions and had Carlisle United under pressure right from the off. They went close on 17 minutes when John Borthwick headed a Phil Linacre cross against the angle of post and bar. The rebound was scrambled clear for a corner, from which Kevan Smith had a header cleared off the line. They took the lead on 21 minutes after Mick Tait had broken up a Carlisle attack. He found Borthwick wide on the right and he played a glorious 40-yard diagonal pass into the path of Drew Coverdale who took the ball in his stride and crashed a shot into the top corner from the edge of the box. Linacre went close on 25 minutes but former Darlington goalkeeper Barry Siddall did well to save. Then Gary Gill broke clear and steered the ball past Siddall, but his shot came back off the foot of the post. United went close to an equaliser on the stroke of half-time when Paul Fitzpatrick hit a speculative 40-yarder that caught on the wind, sailed over Mark Prudhoe, and struck the outside of the far post.

It took Darlington only eight minutes of the second half to increase their lead. Superb control by Andy Toman down the left gave him the time and space to pick out a square ball into Linacre who smashed it first time into the roof of the net from 12 yards out. Gill then hit the post again after a clever one-two with Linacre, before the visitors got back into the game with a goal by Tony Shepherd on 69 minutes. A poor clearance by Smith fell to the former Celtic striker who drilled home from the edge of the box. Shepherd was sent off ten minutes later for foul and abusive language after arguing with the referee John Key. The Quakers made sure of the three points and top spot in the Fourth Division table with a third goal in the last minute. A Coverdale corner was clipped back into the goalmouth by Toman and flicked home from close range by Smith, to make amends for his earlier error.

As I sat at home reading my programme and looking back over the game, I thought that Gary Gill had been excellent during the whole match. Firstly, he struck the woodwork twice but in addition to that, he played his midfield role to perfection.

Looking back, Darlington were lucky to have him at that time, because he was far too good for the Fourth Division.

* * *

Simon Shaw – Career Details

Simon Shaw made 176 appearances in the Football League as a right-back and midfielder for Darlington in the 1990s.

He also went on to play 72 games in the Conference Premier for Doncaster Rovers and was capped for England semi-professional XI while with the club.

Simon also played for Northern Premier League club Barrow and for other non-league teams including Thornaby, Bishop Auckland and Billingham Synthonia where he spent four seasons and scored 24 goals in 104 appearances and took the free kick from which James Magowan scored the only goal of the 2009 Durham Challenge Cup Final.

At the time of writing, Simon is a primary school teacher.

My Memorable Match Involving Simon Shaw
Scunthorpe United v Darlington – 1992/93

I travelled to this match with Ian in his car. After a pub lunch, the pair of us headed to Glanford Park.

We saw the Quakers make a strong start and dominate the early stages. Simon Shaw and Steve O'Shaughnessy both missed early chances as Scunthorpe struggled to get into the game. Shaw had another chance on five minutes when he met a Steve Gaughan cross at the far post, but side-footed his volley over the bar. Shortly after, Gaughan curled a free kick just over the bar from the edge of the box, after Glenn Humphries had fouled Steve Mardenborough.

Darlington took the lead that their early play had deserved with a superb individual goal by Shaw after 23 minutes. He gained possession in his own half and set off towards the United goal. A home defender attempted a tackle just over the halfway line, clipped his heel and dislodged one of the youngster's boots, but with space opening up in front of him, Shaw just kept going. He raced half the length of the field before unleashing a fierce right-footed shot, with his stocking foot, which flew into the bottom corner from 25 yards out. It was Shaw's third goal in five games.

Scunthorpe hit back and managed an equaliser on 32 minutes with their first shot on target. Graham Alexander crossed from the left to giant centre-forward Ian Helliwell, who headed the ball down to Sam Goodacre to fire past Mark Prudhoe from close range. The half ended with chances at both ends. A Gaughan corner was headed towards goal by Kevan Smith but was well saved by then future Darlington player Mark Samways in the home goal. Then at the other end, Goodacre volleyed a good chance wide and Alexander brought a fine save from Prudhoe with Darlington relieved to see Helliwell knock the rebound wide when it looked easier to score.

The second half began with the visitors back in control. On 56 minutes Mardenborough raced through and crashed a shot against the angle of post and bar with Samways well beaten. Four minutes later, the striker had another chance and this time he made no mistake. Racing into the box, he shrugged off his marker and fired past Samways at his near post from an acute angle. The home side tried to hit back and Ian Thompstone twice went close with headers before Goodacre fired high over the bar after a goalmouth scramble. O'Shaughnessy then went close for the Quakers when his long-range shot was tipped over. Mardenborough scored his second of the afternoon in the 85th minute to secure the victory. Shaw floated a superb long ball over the defence and Mardenborough cleverly flicked it over the onrushing Samways and stroked it into the empty net to seal an excellent Darlington victory.

During our journey home, our main topic of conversation was Simon Shaw's goal. It was a goal to store in one's memory bank, that's for sure!

* * *

Peter Kirkham – Career Details

Peter Kirkham was born in Newcastle upon Tyne and began his career as a youngster with his hometown club. He never played first-team football for the Magpies and moved on to Darlington in 1993, making his senior debut on 2 November in the starting 11 for the Third Division match at home to Colchester United. The Quakers won 7-3 and Kirkham made nine more appearances that season, mainly as a substitute. He played in six matches in 1994/95, and left the club at the end of that campaign.

Peter then played in Sweden for Köping FF and also featured back in the UK for teams including Gretna, Blyth Spartans, South Shields, Grantham Town, Chester-le-Street Town, Dunston Federation Brewery, Jarrow – for whom he scored the decisive penalty in the shoot-out that won the club's first Wearside League Trophy, the Shipowners' Charity Cup, in 1995 – Hebburn Town, Consett, Whitley Bay and Washington.

The winger returned to Jarrow in 2006 and was assistant manager to Davy Bell by 2010 and took over as player-manager with Bell becoming his assistant. Kirkham played until 2013 and in January 2016, he again became Bell's assistant when the latter returned to Jarrow as manager.

This is what Peter did after falling out of professional football, in his own words:

'My dream of staying in professional football was over at the age of 22. Shortly after that, I became obsessed about fighting for a better life; with this in mind, and after a lot of planning, I borrowed £3,000 at the age of 27. Four years later, I had turned it into a multi-million pound property portfolio. Then the credit crunch hit and at the age of 38 I lost everything I owned. Once the shock of this had gone, I sat down with my mam and dad and said, "I promise you both, I'm going to get it all back." Within six years I had created a business from scratch and then sold it for millions of pounds.

'I'm now involved with private equity companies that give people the opportunity to gain transformational wealth and have benefitted from one event together with another.

'I was due to retire in March 2023 but I've got too many personal targets to hit. Creating a £100m business is my next goal.'

Talking to Peter was a real insight and I was impressed by his determination to overcome adversity and fight back.

One day in the future, I hope to work with him; who knows what might happen though.

My Memorable Match Involving Peter Kirkham
Darlington v Colchester United – 1993/94

I went with Ian and from our usual vantage point, we saw an absolutely breathtaking game of football.

It took the Quakers only 42 seconds to open the scoring. Gary Himsworth's shot was parried by the keeper but striker Lee Ellison followed up and scored from the rebound. Colchester equalised in the ninth minute through Alan Dickens, but Darlington were back in front on 20 minutes when Robbie Painter fired home – this was the first time we'd scored two goals in a game all season. Gary Chapman added a third after 33 minutes, scoring from close range after a Himsworth corner.

The second half continued in the same free-scoring vein. Painter made it 4-1 after 58 minutes, but Colchester immediately hit back with a second goal by Steve McGavin. Gary Himsworth then took centre stage, clearing a header off his own goal line, then popping up in the opposite goalmouth to stab home and make the score 5-2. Colchester weren't finished and reduced the arrears with a third goal in the 75th minute, this time through Mark Kinsella. Five minutes later, Chapman headed down at the far post for Ellison to score his second of the night and then in the 84th minute, Himsworth crossed for Chapman to fly full length and score with a brilliant diving header to complete the scoring and make the final result an amazing 7-3. It must have been quite some team talk by Alan

Murray, who famously said after the game that he hadn't felt confident of the victory until we were four goals in front with two minutes remaining!

As Ian pushed me to the pub for a quick drink, we both agreed that Gary Himsworth had played really well; I also mentioned that Peter Kirkham, on his debut, had looked promising. He was bombing up the left until he was substituted. I said that he 'looked one for the future'. Unfortunately, during that season, he was used mainly as a substitute and never got a run in the team, which, even looking back now, was a shame because he had unbelievable skills on the ball and in my humble opinion should have been utilised a lot more than he was.

* * *

Michael Oliver – Career Details

Michael Oliver was born in Middlesbrough and began his career in the youth system at his hometown club. He turned professional with them, but his only first-team appearance came on 16 November 1993, as a substitute in the Anglo-Italian Cup against Ancona. In 1994, he signed for Stockport County; the fee was determined by a tribunal. He made his Football League debut for his new club on 28 February 1995, at the age of 19, as a substitute in a 4-0 defeat at Oxford United in the Second Division, and played in 12 of the remaining 14 matches in the 1994/95 season. He was used infrequently in his second season and was released at its end, dropping down two divisions to sign for Darlington.

Michael settled well at Darlington, where he spent four years and played at least 40 matches in each season in all competitions. His last game for the club was in the 2000 Third Division play-off final defeat to Peterborough United. When his contract expired, he left and signed for another Third Division club in Rochdale. He played regularly for two seasons, but his 2002/03 season was disrupted by injury and he was released at its end.

Following his departure from Rochdale, Michael moved into non-league football with Barrow of the Northern

Premier League, and went on to play for other clubs including Spennymoor United, Thornaby, Bishop Auckland Newcastle Blue Star, Gateshead and Durham City.

At the time of writing, Michael is a rigger. His job involves putting in pipelines or subsea structures for oil and gas.

My Memorable Match Involving Michael Oliver
Darlington v Wigan Athletic – 1996/97

I went to this match with Ian. The pair of us took up our usual positions in the East Stand Paddock.

We saw the Quakers make a solid start defensively, only allowing a couple of half chances to the previously free-scoring Wigan attack, who'd scored 12 goals in their first five games. In the 15th minute Colin Greenall flicked on a right-wing corner to John Pender, who headed towards goal, but Phil Brumwell was on hand to clear the ball off the line. Two minutes later, they threatened again. Graeme Jones dribbled past Sean Gregan but goalkeeper Paul Newell saved bravely at his feet just as he was about to shoot. Darlington scored with their first meaningful attempt at goal in the 32nd minute. Michael Oliver, on his debut, and Phil Brumwell combined to set up Gary Twynham, who burst past three defenders as he broke into the box and hit a low right-footed shot which visiting keeper Lee Butler saved but couldn't hold on to. Darren Roberts was the first to react as he hammered the loose ball into the net for his fifth of the season.

The goal gave the home side confidence and allowed them to play some superb passing football after the break to cause their visitors all sorts of problems. They almost added a second goal on 56 minutes when Oliver found the overlapping Brumwell down the right but the full-back fired just past the post. They had a lucky escape on the hour though as Brumwell appeared to bring down Gavin Johnson in the goalmouth as the two players contested a Roberto Martínez free kick, but Wigan's penalty appeals were waved away by referee Richard Poulain. Three minutes later, the hosts were 2-0 ahead. Robbie Blake released Oliver down the right and his first time cross deceived keeper Butler and found its way into the far top corner of the net.

Roberts then had two opportunities to increase the lead when put clear, but on both occasions he allowed defenders to recover and clear the danger. He made up for this in the 82nd minute though, when he played a large part in the build-up to a superb third goal. He picked up the ball in his own half and played it forwards to Anthony Carss who played a first-time return pass into the centre-forward's path down the left wing, from where he crossed perfectly for Blake to side-foot home on the volley from six yards out. Greenall pulled a goal back for the visitors with a header from a corner two minutes into injury time, but it was too little too late for Wigan, who ended the night a well beaten side.

I can remember thinking as Ian pushed me to the town centre for a few drinks that Michael Oliver looked to have been a great signing. He was certainly my man of the match in what was a really good Darlington display.

* * *

Gary Twynham – Career Details

Gary Twynham began his career at Manchester United. He also played as a midfielder for Darlington when they were in the Football League.

After leaving the Quakers, Gary featured for Gateshead, Grantham Town, Lincoln City (loan), Hednesford United, Macclesfield Town, Haverfordwest County, Port Talbot Town and Barry Town.

My Memories of Gary Twynham

I first met Gary when he played for Darlington in 1996. However, as happens lots of times in life, we lost touch for several years after he had left the club.

We met up when Robbie Painter and I arranged a charity football match at Northallerton Town. Gary very kindly drove up from South Wales to play. I never forgot him for doing that.

Once again, we lost touch until 2021 when I got a message out of the blue from him on Facebook.

Since then, Gary has supported whatever I do with great enthusiasm. He purchased two of my books, *Give Them Wings* and *One Hundred of the Best*. As well as this he managed to obtain pictures of Mike England with both books, for which I was really grateful.

At the time of writing, Gary is an engineer for a telecommunications company.

This time, we have remained in regular contact and I regard him as a friend.

* * *

Neil Wainwright – Career Details

Neil Wainwright began his career as a trainee at Wrexham in July 1996, making 11 league appearances in two seasons before joining Sunderland for £100,000 in July 1998. He made only two substitute appearances in the league and six in the League Cup for the Black Cats before being loaned to Darlington in February 2000 for the rest of the 2000/01 season. Neil joined Halifax Town on loan in October 2000 for three months and then returned to Darlington in a permanent transfer for a fee of £50,000 in August 2001, where he made over 270 appearances in all competitions and was the club's player of the year in 2006/07, but after making only six appearances at the start of the 2007/08 season he joined Shrewsbury Town on a one-month loan in October 2007. He later joined Mansfield Town in March 2008 until the end of the campaign but was recalled by Darlington a month later having made five appearances for the Stags.

Following Darlington's failure to gain promotion from League Two in 2007/08, Wainwright was one of several players surprisingly released by the club in May 2008. He joined Morecambe in June 2008 and excelled in a left wing-back role before his season was cut short by an injury. In 2011, he was released.

On 28 February 2012, Neil rejoined Darlington who at that time were in severe financial straits and battling relegation from the Conference National following a ten-point deduction for entering administration in December 2011. He had been playing for Kendal Town prior to his signing for the Quakers, making his league debut on 27 September 2011 and scoring in a 3-3 draw with Marine. Neil made two more league appearances, alongside seven cup matches, before leaving Kendal in November 2011. He made his third Darlington debut on 3 March 2012, in a 1-0 home loss to Stockport County; he wore the number 26 shirt and was replaced by Clark Keltie in the 67th minute. He left the Quakers in the summer of 2012 as the club were relegated and folded, later to reform as Darlington 1883 in the Northern League.

For the start of the 2012/13 season Wainwright signed as a player for Northern Premier League club Lancaster City, taking over as joint manager in October 2012 before leaving in February 2013.

At the time of writing Neil is head of youth at Morecambe.

My Memorable Match Involving Neil Wainwright
Darlington v Rochdale 1999/2000

I went to this match with Ian and his friend Simon. After visiting Strikers Bar which was situated in the new East Stand, Simon sat with me in the disabled area and Ian went in the Tin Shed.

Simon and I witnessed a brilliant Darlington performance. By half-time they were 3-1 up and we added another goal to our tally by full time. The scorers were Peter Duffield (two), Marco Gabbiadini and Neil Wainwright, whose loan had been extended for a further month, much to my delight. Having been substituted the latter got a standing ovation after putting in a scintillating display, the highlight of which was the cross that led to Duffield's second goal.

All of us left the ground in a buoyant frame of mind, eagerly awaiting the visit of our next opponents.

Ian and I both agreed that Neil had been excellent throughout the whole time he was on the pitch. He'd literally torn the Rochdale defence apart in one of the best displays I've ever seen from a winger to this day.

* * *

Neil Heaney – Career Details

Neil Heaney began his career as a winger with Arsenal before making 61 appearances in the Premier League for Southampton. He played in the Football League for Manchester City, Hartlepool United, Cambridge United, Charlton Athletic, Bristol City, Darlington and Plymouth Argyle, and also had a spell in the Scottish Premier League with Dundee United.

He was also capped six times by England's under-21s in 1992.

After retiring in 2002 Neil left football and became CEO of Judicare, an English firm of solicitors that deals with international legal issues and is known particularly for recovering monies invested into problematic property abroad, based partly on his own problems investing in Spanish property.

My Memorable Match Involving Neil Heaney

Darlington v Carlisle United – 1999/2000

Ian and I witnessed a really good Darlington performance from our usual vantage point.

The home team started strongly and completely overran the visitors' defence who relied on former Quakers goalkeeper Michael Ingham to keep Darlington out. Neil Heaney had an early shot blocked, then on 16 minutes Craig Russell hit a fierce left-footed volley which Ingham managed to save with his legs. Phil Brumwell then had an effort blocked and Ingham saved superbly from Marco Gabbiadini's follow-up. Heaney, who was having an excellent game, fired two long-range shots just wide before Gabbiadini saw his curling free kick touched over the bar by the overworked Carlisle keeper. Ingham was in action yet again to keep out another Russell effort, then Brian Atkinson blazed over the bar from a couple of yards out. Just when it looked like the Cumbrians might hold out until half-time, the Quakers grabbed the lead in stoppage time, when Brumwell and Gabbiadini combined well down the right to set up Russell who fired a left-footed shot into the net from just inside the area.

The hosts finished the game off with two quick goals at the start of the second half. On 47 minutes substitute Gary Himsworth fired in a shot that was blocked but the ball ran loose to Gabbiadini who bundled it home from close range. Two minutes later it was 3-0 when Heaney was hauled down in full flight by Peter Clark who was immediately red-carded for a professional foul. Gabbiadini curled the resulting free kick around the wall and into the top corner. Ingham continued his fine evening's work by saving from Craig Liddle, Himsworth and Gabbiadini twice before Lee Nogan missed a sitter with his first touch after replacing Russell. Completely against the run of play, Carlisle pulled a goal back on 77 minutes when Steve Tutill was dispossessed by Paul Harries inside his own area and the Cumbrian based player slotted past Andy Collett in the home goal.

As my friend pushed me back to his car, my main thought was what a fine game Neil Heaney had played. He was really unlucky with three shots at goal and also he won the free kick that led to Darlington's third goal. In addition, his overall wing play had been excellent throughout the whole match.

* * *

Mark Kilty – Career Details

Mark Kilty played 23 league games, scoring once in seven years for Darlington between 1997 and 2004.

Mark's professional career was cut short by injury aged just 23 after suffering two ruptured anterior cruciate knee ligaments in his right knee and also a tear to his left patella tendon. In his injury-ravaged career he was operated on eight times. After three years of physiotherapy and rehabilitation, unfortunately he retired.

Alan Walsh – Darlington's joint-record goalscorer and one of my all-time favourite players

David Speedie – One of the best players I've seen at Darlington in over 50 years

Kevan Smith – I have two words to describe this guy: 'Mr Darlington'.

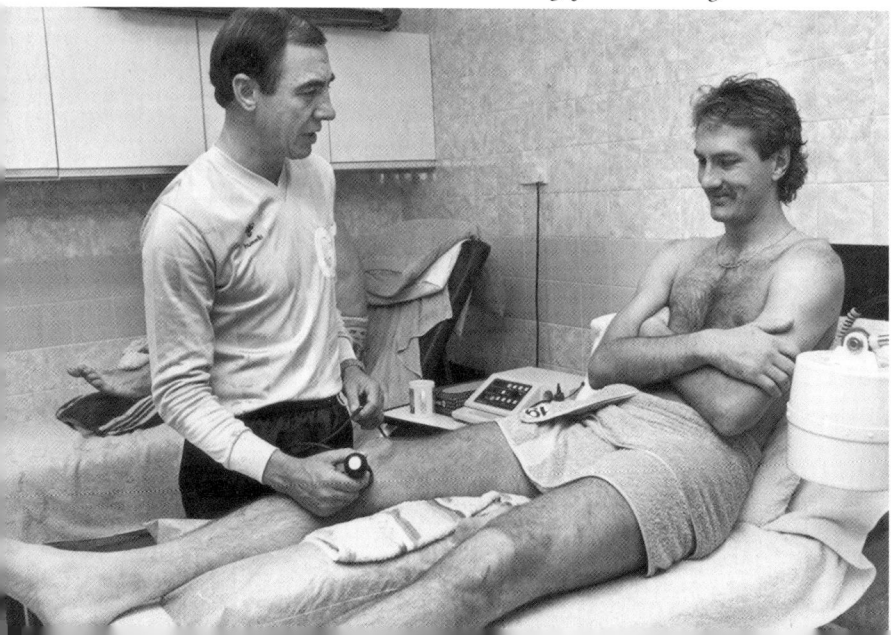

Neil Wainwright – I loved watching Neil bomb down the wing during his three spells at Darlington

Michael Smith – I really admire this guy because whilst at Darlington, he contracted meningitis, yet he recovered and has had a really good football career! That takes guts!

Jarrett Rivers – my favourite post-2012 player

Stephen Thompson – Darlington's joint-record goalscorer and without doubt, the best post 2012 striker the club has had

Will Hatfield – One of my favourite post 2012-players

With help from the PFA, he graduated from the University of Salford in 2009 with a degree in physiotherapy.

Mark is now a health care consultant, an author, and founder of PhysioBlu Ltd based in Team Valley in his native north-east. He has appeared on BBC, ITV, Sky Sports, Sky Sports News and has been seen in *The Journal*, the *Evening Chronicle* and the *Northern Echo* and is the master of the bow and arrow technique along with the moonwalk which now has the 'Kilty' trademark.

My Memorable Match Involving Mark Kilty
Darlington v Shrewsbury Town – 2000/01

I went to this match with my buddy Ian and we were lucky enough to see an excellent Darlington performance.

The two of us saw the home side make a good start and take the lead after 11 minutes. Craig Liddle joined in an attack and hit a low cross from the right. The ball bounced across the goalmouth and found Olivier Bernard ghosting in beyond the far post to side-foot home. Two minutes later it was nearly 2-0 as Liddle found Glenn Naylor breaking into the box but the striker lobbed just over. Shrewsbury almost equalised on 17 minutes when former Sunderland winger Sam Aiston threatened, but Peter Keen in the Darlington goal got down to block his effort with his feet.

The hosts scored their second on 24 minutes with a superb breakaway goal after defending a Shrewsbury free kick. Adam Reed cleared the ball from his own box down the left wing. Richard Hodgson made progress, beat his man, and crossed to the far post to John Williams, who pulled the ball back into the path of Mark Kilty, who had run virtually the full length of the pitch to fire into the top corner for his first goal for the club. The Quakers were well on top now and playing some superb football. In a rare attack for the visitors Nigel Jemson hit a fierce free kick which Keen did well to hold. However, it was the home side who looked much more likely to score again. They did so a minute before half-time and once again Liddle was involved. He found Williams down the right-hand edge of the penalty area and he squared the ball across the six-yard box to Naylor who volleyed home at the near post.

Shrewsbury made two substitutions at half-time in an effort to change the game and they started the second half brightly. Aiston broke into the box and fired just wide, then Luke Rodgers had an opportunity but he shot wide when put under pressure by Liddle. Darlington soon regained control though and played out the remainder of the game in a comfortable fashion. They went close to a fourth goal late on when Shrews keeper Paul Edwards came out of his area to challenge Naylor and lost the ball. The striker then curled a shot towards goal from out wide on the right but full-back Ross Davidson got back on to the line to clear. That turned out to be the last real chance of the match.

As I sat at home reading my programme, in my mind I looked back at Mark Kilty's goal. As I mentioned, he ran almost the full length of the pitch to score. Also, his general midfield performance during the whole game had been excellent.

Looking back now, it was probably one of his best appearances for the club.

* * *

Michael Cummins – Career Details

Michael Cummings started his career with Middlesbrough in 1996, where he stayed for four years. In 2000, he moved to Port Vale and made over 250 appearances for the club in a six-year stay, picking up a Football League Trophy winners' medal in 2001.

Between 2006 and 2008 Michael played for Darlington. However, in 2008 he joined Rotherham United. Two years later the midfielder was transferred to Grimsby Town, before signing for Gateshead in May 2011.

Over the course of his career Michael scored 67 goals in 588 league and cup appearances. He has also appeared for the Republic of Ireland under-21 team and played all of Ireland's five games at the 1997 FIFA World Youth Championship.

He turned to coaching after retiring as a player and twice took charge as caretaker/manager at Gateshead. He worked as a coach at the club before taking up a coaching role at York City from 2019 to 2021.

My Memorable Match Involving Michael Cummins
Bury v Darlington – 2007/08

I made the trip to this match on the train with Ian.

To our surprise, we arrived in Manchester right on time (almost every time we'd used this service, it had been late) and caught the Metrolink to Bury. One comment on this part of our journey: both the platforms and indeed the trams were really accessible for wheelchair users and Ian managed to get me aboard our particular tram without any problems at all.

Before we knew it, we were at our destination. Our first port of call was the George, a pub in the centre of Bury, where we enjoyed a pint before heading to the ground in a cab. We'd have stayed longer in the George but they didn't sell food, hence our decision to leave.

On arrival at the stadium we went to the supporters' bar where we bumped into John Gray who had caught an earlier train than us. John, like me, thought Darlington would win, but I knew that it wouldn't be an easy game as Bury were deep in relegation trouble and needed the points, albeit for different reasons than we did.

Luckily they sold food in the bar and after we'd finished eating Ian went to collect the complimentary tickets that my friend Neil Wainwright had said he'd leave for us. Within a few minutes he returned with the tickets in his hand which we were eternally grateful for.

After another pint, we left the bar and headed to the away end from where I noticed that Neil was among the substitutes which pleased me, and probably more so him, come to think of it!

Darlington started like a house on fire and took the lead after only five minutes. Ricky Ravenhill was fouled in the penalty area and the referee immediately awarded a spot-kick.

With both our penalty takers, Clark Keltie and Richie Foran, out injured it was left to Guylain Ndumbu-Nsungu to take the kick. He blasted the ball past Bury keeper Darren Randolph for his first goal since he had rejoined Darlington and his seventh of the season (the other six were scored while he was on loan at Bradford City from Gillingham). After the goal, the Quakers missed a host of chances to make the game safe. Firstly Neil Austin put through Kevin Gall but his shot was weak and was easily saved by the keeper. Ian Miller then headed over an Austin free kick. Finally, Ndumbu-Nsungu blasted the ball over the bar from about six yards out. The home side's best chance of the first half fell to former York City striker Andy Bishop, but his well-struck shot hit the bottom of the post with David Stockdale well beaten. I have to say, however, I was disappointed that we were only 1-0 up at the interval.

The visitors started the second half as they did the first and Gall could have scored three goals within the first five minutes. His first chance came after he was set up by Neil Wainwright, who was on for the injured Julian Joachim, but he prodded the ball wide following the cross. A couple of minutes later he headed against the bar following good work by Austin. Finally Randolph clawed away his goalbound header following another excellent run and cross by Austin. However, the pressure eventually paid off and Darlington doubled their lead after 67 minutes when Michael Cummins headed home Gall's corner.

Following the goal, Bury pressed forward and were rewarded with a consolation goal in the 87th minute when Efe Sodje scored from Elliott Bennett's corner. In the very last minute, the hosts almost equalised but Stephen Foster cleared Bishop's shot off the line to ensure the three points headed back to Darlington.

I have to say that I thought that without doubt, the Quakers had deserved their win and I'd been impressed with Michael Cummins's performance as we headed home, after what had been an excellent day out.

* * *

Jason Kennedy – Career Details

Jason Kennedy started his career at Middlesbrough. He made his debut for the north-east club in the 2004/05 season, against Fulham. He made six appearances, four of which were as a substitute, in 2005/06. He also participated in Middlesbrough's UEFA Cup run that season against Litex Lovech, playing the full game.

Kennedy was handed a two-year contract in 2005 by manager Steve McClaren. He joined Scottish Football League club Livingston in August 2007 on a six-month loan deal.

He made another loan move in 2008, this time to League Two side Darlington. On 10 May 2008, Kennedy scored the first goal in the League Two play-off semi-final first leg between Darlington and Rochdale. Darlington went on to win the match 2-1. However, in the second leg he missed his spot kick in a penalty shoot-out, sending the Dale through to the final. On 30 May Kennedy signed a two-year permanent deal with the Quakers.

On 20 May 2009 Jason signed a two-year contract with Rochdale. He scored his first goal for the club on 28 August 2010 in a 3-1 win against Brentford, but was sent off as celebrating with the fans earned him a second yellow card. He followed this up with goals against Milton Keynes Dons, Huddersfield Town and Charlton Athletic and ended the season with four goals. He played his final game for the club on 27 April 2013, helping Rochdale to a 1-0 win against Plymouth Argyle. He left having made over 200 appearances during a four-year spell and was part of the 2009/10 promotion-winning team.

In July 2013, Jason signed for Bradford City on a free transfer following the expiry of his contract, on a two-year deal. He had almost signed for the club during the previous transfer window and rejected the chance to stay at Rochdale, as well as an offer from Hartlepool United, to sign for the Bantams. He made his league debut on 5 October in a 2-0 win away to Walsall.

On 24 January, Kennedy moved back to Rochdale on loan until the end of the 2013/14 season.

In March 2015, Kennedy completed a one-month loan deal at League Two club Carlisle United. He made a bright start with his new club, scoring his first goal in only his second start, a 2-0 away victory over Northampton.

It was announced that Kennedy would leave Bradford at the end of the season and he returned to Carlisle the same week, signing a permanent two-year deal. He was released by Carlisle at the end of the 2018/19 season.

Following a successful trial, Kennedy signed for Hartlepool United on 18 July 2019.

Half way through the season, Jason signed for National League North side Spennymoor Town on loan until the end of the campaign. Following his release from his parent club, he became player-coach at the County Durham Club in May 2021.

At the time of writing, Jason is playing in the Northern Premier League for Marske United.

My Memorable Match Involving Jason Kennedy

Darlington v Rochdale, play-off semi-final first leg – 2007/08

I attended this game with one of my PAs. It was broadcast live on Sky Sports and I wondered if many fans would stay away and watch it in the pub. I needn't have worried as a crowd of 8,057, the biggest attendance of the season by far, were in the stadium.

The two of us witnessed a brilliant Darlington performance, one that had us on the edge of our seats.

Jason Kennedy scored one of the best goals ever seen at the Arena in the first half. He received the ball from Leeds United loanee Ben Parker and beat his man before curling it around the Rochdale keeper Tommy Lee and into the net. It was truly a brilliant goal, one that I wouldn't forget in a hurry. Minutes later, Alan White headed wide following a good run and cross from Rob Purdie. The game continued to ebb and flow and Darlo were excellent value for their lead at the interval.

The Quakers were made to pay for several missed second-half opportunities when the visitors equalised in the 70th minute. Chris Dagnall got the ball on the Darlo left and hit it from 25 yards, but unfortunately it struck Stephen Foster on his thigh before ending up in the back of the net. Darlington, to their credit, didn't let their heads drop and took the lead in the second minute of injury time. Neil Wainwright swung in a free kick from the left, and fellow substitute Miller outjumped everyone to plant a header firmly past Lee. The home fans, including PA Ann and I, went wild. Shortly after the goal the final whistle went.

After the match, we met Ian in the bar; the two of us couldn't believe how good Jason Kennedy's goal was. One thing for sure, I will never forget it!

* * *

Chris Emms – Career Details

Chris Emms started his career at Middlesbrough and played for their junior teams. Unfortunately, he didn't make their first team and eventually signed for Spennymoor Town, then moved to Blyth Spartans in July 2011. A few months later Chris was on the move again, this time to Billingham Synthonia.

In July 2012, the winger signed for Darlington. He stayed with the Quakers for a year before taking a break from football.

Chris later played for several Northern League clubs including Crook Town, Northallerton Town, Billingham Town and Bishop Auckland.

My Memorable Match Involving Chris Emms
Darlington v Consett – 2012/13

I went to this match with Ian in his car. Once at Heritage Park, the pair of us went to the March Hare where we had a pub lunch. While in there, we bumped into John Gray and Richard Jones. They both thought that Darlington would win the game easily. I agreed, having seen Consett earlier in the season; they looked poor when we had beaten them.

After our lunch, Ian and I said our goodbyes to John and Richard before heading to the ground.

The pair of us were lucky enough to see an excellent Darlington performance.

The Quakers scored with only 15 seconds on the clock when Amar Purewal collected a long pass from Stephen Harrison before beating former Middlesbrough – and future Darlington – keeper Peter Jameson with a fine finish. The home side dominated proceedings with David Dowson and Purewal going close on several occasions. The second goal came in the 37th minute when Dowson managed to poke the ball past Jameson despite colliding with him. Two minutes later, Dowson got his second goal and Darlington's third when he blasted the ball home following an excellent pull back from winger Adam Nicholls.

The home side added a fourth goal shortly after the restart when Chris Emms received a pass from Nicholls before chipping the ball over Jameson from all of 20 yards for what was a brilliant finish. Consett came back at Darlington when former Hartlepool and Gateshead striker Michael Mackay had a shot well saved by Jack Norton in the home side's goal. Norton also had to be on his toes when he palmed away a well-struck effort from Stephen Callen. Just as they had in the first half, the home team dominated the match and it came as no surprise when substitute Shaun Reay grabbed the fifth goal; again Adam Nicholls was the provider, he playing an excellent pass in for the striker who then rounded Jameson before shooting into the empty net to round off an excellent performance from Martin Gray's men.

As Ian pushed me back to the car, we both agreed that if Chris Emms's goal had been on *Match of the Day*, it would have been the goal of the month, without a doubt. In addition, I said that the winger had been excellent throughout the game.

* * *

Leon Scott – Career Details
Leon was a product of the Middlesbrough academy, and has played for Peterlee, Dunston, Newcastle Blue Star, Whitby

Town (twice), Harrogate Town, Shildon and Norton & Stockton Ancients. He is a strong and powerful player who was one of the first signings of the Darlington FC renaissance in the 2012/13 season and finished the season with ten league goals from centre midfield.

In 2013/14, he played mainly as a central midfielder, and was injured in the opening minutes of the play-off semi-final against Ramsbottom. He was a regular in the 2014/15 and 2015/16 promotion-winning seasons, and collected two more promotion winners' medals, to add to his Northern League one which he won in 2012/13.

At the time of writing, Leon plays for West Auckland Town.

My Memorable Match Involving Leon Scott
Billingham Synthonia v Darlington – 2012/13

I went to this match with Ian in his car and the pair of us witnessed a very good Darlington performance, eventually.

After having lunch in Stockton, we headed for the ground, Central Avenue. The home team surprisingly held a half-time lead given to them by a speculative cross by Danny Johnson. Darlington had been far the better of the two teams in the first half but had missed several gilt-edged chances. To be honest, striker Stephen Thompson could have had three or four goals.

As I drank my pint during the break, I can remember saying to Ian that maybe it wasn't going to be our day. However, I needn't have worried.

Captain Marvel Gary Brown equalised from a free kick just after the restart and from then on, it was plain sailing for the visitors. Former Billingham Synthonia player Chris Emms came on as substitute and scored with his first touch after 68 minutes, then shortly after, full-back Darren Richardson set up Thompson for the third. Leon Scott completed the scoring when he blasted the ball home from the edge of the box for his eighth goal in as many games. The goal sealed what was an excellent second-half display from the Quakers.

My main memory of the match was Scott's performance. He must have covered every blade of grass and certainly deserved his goal.

* * *

Martin Gray – Career Details

Born in Stockton-on-Tees, Martin Gray's main position was in midfield, but he played in all outfield positions during his career. He started his career as a trainee at Sunderland in 1990 and stayed with them until 1996 when he made a £100,000 transfer to Oxford United, then from there he was transferred to Darlington in 1999.

Gray and Neil Maddison took over as joint caretaker managers following the popular David Hodgson's departure from Darlington in 2006. Former Doncaster Rovers manager Dave Penney took over on 30 October 2006, with Gray remaining at the club as his assistant manager.

He once again took over as caretaker manager on 30 April 2009 after Penney moved to Oldham Athletic. With Darlington in administration, he was released on 7 May, along with other members of the club's staff, and joined up with Penney again as his assistant later that month. Gray took over as caretaker manager for the final match of the 2009/10 season after Penney left Oldham on 6 May 2010. Martin also departed on 2 June after being unsuccessful in his application for the permanent manager's position.

On 28 May 2012, Martin was appointed as the manager of Darlington on a two-year contract. In his first season in charge, he guided the club to the Northern League Division One title. In his next campaign, the Quakers finished as Northern Premier League Division One North runners-up, but they lost in the play-off semi-final to Ramsbottom United. However, the following season, Martin guided the club to another second-placed finish in the division, and on this occasion they secured promotion by beating Bamber Bridge 2-0 in the play-off final. Twelve months later, Darlington won the 2015/16 Northern

Premier League Premier Division title and clinched promotion to National League North. They finished fifth in their first season but were unable to participate in the play-offs due to ground grading issues.

Gray resigned from his post as manager on 1 October 2017.

He was appointed manager of newly relegated National League North club York City on 1 October 2017, with Penney assisting him as sporting director. He left the club on 19 August 2018 when the club opted against renewing his contract, with the team eighth in the table five matches into the 2018/19 season.

My Memorable Match Involving Martin Gray

Darlington v Team Northumbria – 2012/13

I went to the Team Northumbria match at Heritage Park, Bishop Auckland, with Ian, knowing that if Darlington won they'd clinch promotion to Division One North of the Northern Premier League.

The ground was packed to the rafters and Darlington missed loads of gilt-edged chances before eventually going behind just before half-time. However the goal appeared to make the home side play with more of a sense of urgency and they equalised shortly after through a well-taken goal by Chris Emms. It was certainly a relief to have my pint up in the bar during the interval knowing that we were on level terms with our visitors especially after witnessing them beat the Quakers earlier that season.

Darlington started the second half very much in the same way as they had ended the first. It came as no surprise to the pair of us early in the half when striker Amar Purewal brilliantly headed home following an excellent run and cross from right-back Stephen Harrison. The Quakers continued to dominate the match but were denied by a mixture of good goalkeeping and poor finishing by their forwards. However, they weren't to be denied for ever and Purewal made sure of the victory in injury time after running on to a through ball from Kerry Hedley and slotting past the visiting keeper. A few seconds later, the final whistle went which meant Darlington had completed the first step on their long journey back up the football pyramid by clinching promotion and winning the Northern League title.

The scenes post-match were brilliant with manager Martin Gray celebrating with his players and indeed the fans.

After watching the celebrations, Ian and I left the ground happy in the knowledge that we had clinched promotion. I never have forgotten Martin Gray celebrating with everyone. Like many incidents regarding Darlington Football Club, it is etched in my mind for ever.

* * *

Adam Mitchell – Career Details

Adam began his career as a schoolboy at Sunderland, and steadily made his way through the ranks until he made his debut for the first team at Tottenham in May 2013, when he came on as a substitute for former Darlington striker Danny Graham. He was a regular in the reserves in 2013/14, but he was loaned out to Harrogate Town and then Darlington near the end of the season and was eventually released. After trials at several clubs in the summer of 2014, he signed a two-year contract with the Quakers.

After leaving Darlington in 2016, Adam joined Spennymoor Town.

My Memorable Match Involving Adam Mitchell
Darlington v Mossley – 2015/16

Once again, I went with Ian and we saw an absolutely brilliant performance from winger Adam Mitchell.

The Quakers made the most of the wind advantage and took the lead after just four minutes. Gary Brown put the ball into the box from the right, and in the scramble that followed, Mitchell drove his shot through a crowd of players and into the net. Darlington scored a second after 13 minutes, after Mitchell intercepted the ball in midfield and found Tom Portas down the right. Mitchell raced into the box and timed his run perfectly to sweep Portas's return pass into the bottom corner. It was almost 3-0 a few minutes later when Terry Galbraith's corner sailed over everyone and Nathan Cartman side-footed wide from a couple of yards out.

Just beyond the 20-minute mark, Mossley had a penalty appeal turned down when Sam Robinson went down under a challenge by Alan White, but the referee waved play on. Cartman had a difficult chance a few minutes later when a Leon Scott header sent him running clear, and with his back almost to goal he tried to flick the ball over the keeper, but it went over the bar.

The hosts scored another goal on 33 minutes when striker Graeme Armstrong unleashed a terrific shot towards goal from the edge of the box that Mossley keeper Liam Flynn parried, but the striker was quick to seize on the rebound and fire home, while the defence appealed for handball. Just prior to half-time, it was almost 4-0 when Portas's square pass found Armstrong, who hit the ball in his stride and produced an excellent fingertip save out of Flynn.

Despite playing against the wind in the second half, Darlington almost scored in the 48th minute when White touched Galbraith's inswinging free kick just wide. The visitors pulled a goal back on 58 minutes when Thompson caught a Mossley attacker as he cleared the ball but, amazingly, the referee awarded a penalty. Mike Fish sent Peter Jameson the wrong way from the spot. Darlington immediately responded at the other end when Cartman neatly laid the ball off for Galbraith to cross into the middle, but unfortunately, the striker's header was touched over by Flynn. Not to be outdone, Jameson pulled off a good save when a corner was cleared as far as Andy Keogh, who hit the ball into the ground and the Darlington keeper flew to his right and held on to the ball. As the game drew to a close, Jameson made another good save, this time from point-blank range, from Rio Ahmadi's header, but that was his last busy moment as the Quakers ran down the clock to ensure that they held on to the precious three points.

As my friend drove me home, I thought that Adam Mitchell had his best game for the club and his two goals, and indeed his wing play, were the difference between the two sides.

* * *

Phil Turnbull – Career Details

Phil Turnbull joined Hartlepool United's youth system in 2003 and was a member of the teams that enjoyed successful Dallas Cup campaigns in 2004 and 2005. He began to establish himself in the reserve team over the next couple of years, while still with the youth setup. He joined Northern Premier League Premier Division club Gateshead on loan in December 2005, making his debut in a 0-0 home draw with Radcliffe Borough on 17 December. He made five appearances before returning to Hartlepool in February 2006.

The midfielder was given his first professional contract on 4 July 2006. He made his first and only appearance for their first team after he started in the 3-1 win over League One team Rotherham United in the Football League Trophy first round on 17 October 2006. He joined Blyth Spartans of Conference North on 22 January 2007 on a one-month loan and made 11 appearances for the club. He was released by Hartlepool in May 2007.

Phil was signed by Conference Premier League club York City on 6 July 2007. A dislocated shoulder picked up in a pre-season friendly against Frickley Athletic in July 2007 resulted in a six-month lay-off with injury. His York City debut came on 12 January 2008 as a 66th-minute substitute in their 0-0 draw at home to Grays Athletic in the FA Trophy second round.

Having failed to establish himself in the York team under manager Colin Walker, Turnbull rejoined Gateshead on a one-month loan in February 2008 and made his debut against Witton Albion. He agreed a permanent contract with the Heed on 11 March 2008 after he was released by York. He scored his first career goal on 1 April 2008 in Gateshead's 2-0 win over Prescot Cables at Valerie Park. Phil finished the season with 18 appearances and one goal for Gateshead as they achieved promotion to the Conference North via the play-offs. The team achieved a second successive promotion, this time to the Conference Premier, after beating AFC Telford United in the 2009 Conference North play-off final, Turnbull finishing the season with 49 appearances and two goals. He agreed a new one-year contract with the club in May 2012 to cover the 2012/13 season. Phil made his 300th appearance for Gateshead on 21 December 2013 in a 4-2 defeat away to Luton Town. He left Gateshead by mutual consent on 29 June 2015 to become a physical education teacher at a school in Sunderland.

Turnbull moved into part-time football when signing for newly promoted Northern Premier League Premier Division club Darlington on 29 June 2015. He played in 35 of the Quakers' 46 league matches in his first season as Darlington finished as champions and were promoted to National League North. He was again a regular as Darlington finished fifth in National League North in 2016/17, scoring his first goal in a 2-0 home win over Gloucester City on 14 January 2017. Although finishing in a play-off position, as mentioned previously, they were denied entry to the play-offs due to their Blackwell Meadows ground not meeting seating requirements.

On 5 October 2017, Turnbull and Gary Brown were appointed joint caretaker managers of Darlington, following the departure of Martin Gray to York City. They remained in charge until Tommy Wright became manager, achieving their only victory in their third and final match in charge, on 21 October 2017 against Bradford Park Avenue.

On 25 May 2018, the midfielder left Darlington to join his hometown team South Shields. He made 94 appearances in all competitions before leaving after the 2020/21 season when the end of his contract coincided with the club moving to a full-time training structure. However, Phil remained in part-time football with Northern Premier League Division One East club Dunston UTS.

My Memorable Match Involving Phil Turnbull
Darlington v Bradford Park Avenue – 2016/17

Ian and I witnessed Phil Turnbull's and Gary Brown's final match as joint caretaker managers in this encounter on what was a very wet and windy day.

The two of us were barely in our places when Darlington took the lead after just 92 seconds. Terry Galbraith played a lovely ball up the left for Josh Gillies to help on for Leon Scott to whip into the middle, Nathan Cartman got a touch with a diving header and Bradford Park Avenue defender Graham Kelly put it into his own goal. The Quakers kept the pressure going in the wet and windy conditions and Turnbull had a powerful shot deflected wide from the edge of the box. Bradford had their first real chance on 15 minutes, when the ball came into the box for Adam Boyes to turn, but he pulled his effort well wide. A few minutes later, it was almost 2-0 to the hosts when Turnbull floated a free kick in from the right, and the ball took a flick off a defender's head and dropped just wide of the post. Darlington had another opportunity when midfielder Tom Portas laid the ball back for Stephen Thompson to drive low towards goal, but a defender blocked it on the six-yard line. The visitors tried to put some pressure on the home side's defence, but they dealt comfortably with it, until the 37th minute when Boyes had a shot on the turn deflected wide.

The wind and rain didn't let up in the second half, much to everyone's discomfort. Park Avenue had a chance at the start of the second period. An inswinging free kick was whipped in from the right, and Boyes headed straight into Adam Bartlett's hands when he should have done better.

The Quakers went 2-0 up on 54 minutes. Dave Syers was fouled on the left, level with the 18-yard line; Gillies curled the free kick into the middle over everyone and it dropped into the net at the far post. They nearly got another shortly after when Syers burst down the right and he tried to squeeze the ball in at the near post, but fired into the side netting. Bradford almost pulled one back when a Darlington defender cleared a right-wing cross as far as Mark Ross, whose right-footed blast was well saved by Bartlett. It was very nearly 3-0 when Syers had a shot blocked, but he chipped the ball inside for midfielder and former Middlesbrough player Joe Wheatley to fire left-footed just wide. Darlington kept pressing and substitute Harvey Saunders then made a great run into the box, kept the ball in and set up Syers, whose shot was blocked. Bradford poured men forward in the closing stages and an effort by Johnson was well turned over the bar by Bartlett. However, with a minute left on the clock, Johnson headed in a left wing cross to cause some nervous moments.

Once I'd arrived home and thought about the match, I honestly thought that Darlington had deserved to win. Dave Syers was brilliant in midfield. But my lasting memory from the day was Phil Turnbull and Gary Brown hugging each other at the end of the match. It's another football-related scene that I'll never forget.

* * *

Jarrett Rivers – Career Details

Jarrett Rivers played youth football for Middlesbrough. After he was released, he began working in a factory, something he later reflected on, 'I quit after one day because it made me realise I did not want to do that for the rest of my life, so I have worked hard in football ever since.'

After spending the 2013/14 season with Whitley Bay, Jarrett joined Blyth Spartans. He combined his non-league career with a job in his mother's newsagents shop. After impressing in Blyth's FA Cup run the following season, including scoring the winner in their second-round victory against Hartlepool United, he went on trial with Oldham Athletic in January 2015. Unfortunately, nothing became of that opportunity. Jarrett, however, was named Northern Premier League Young Player of the Season for 2014/15 and in May 2015 he signed a one-year professional contract with an option for a second year with Blackpool, newly relegated to League One. The winger made ten League One appearances for his new club, mainly as a substitute, but the option for a further year was not taken up and he rejoined Blyth in August 2016.

Jarrett signed for Darlington in May 2019 and at the time of writing, as well as playing for the first team, he is also manager at the club's academy.

My Memorable Match Involving Jarrett Rivers
Darlington v Kidderminster Harriers – 2019/20

I went to this match with Chris, my PA. The pair of us witnessed a hard working Darlington performance, against a full-time team.

The visitors forced a corner in the first minute, but after the ball was initially cleared, Darlington keeper Liam Connell managed to catch it under pressure. The Quakers replied almost immediately with a good run down the right by Jarrett Rivers, who got into the box and fired across the face of goal and just past the post. On six minutes the ball was switched from right to left for Adam Campbell to run inside and hit a right-footed shot just over the bar from the edge of the area. After about ten minutes, Darlington defender Ben Hedley picked the ball up on the halfway line and from fully 30 yards hit a powerful right-footed shot that Kidderminster keeper Cameron Gregory just managed to tip over the bar. Shortly after, Joe Wheatley then won the ball and set Hedley up again in a more central position, but this time he fired over the top.

The home side continued to press and on 16 minutes striker Tyrone O'Neill picked the ball up on the edge of the box, turned quickly, and fired wide of the post. Another chance came on 20 minutes when Rivers left two defenders in his wake on the right and found O'Neill, who pulled the ball back for Campbell to have a shot blocked. The game was fairly even after that, until the home side took the lead on 40 minutes when O'Neill nodded a Hedley free kick down for Omar Holness to his right and he cleverly flicked the ball on for Rivers to run through and slot into the bottom corner for his second goal of the season.

There was a chance for 2-0 on 50 minutes when Campbell charged down a clearance by Gregory, but he couldn't quite turn the ball home. The visitors almost equalised a few minutes later when Ashley Hemmings found space 25 yards out on the right, turned and struck a low shot that Connell held well on the line. Stephen Thompson came on as substitute on 70 minutes and with his first touch he struck a 30-yarder which flew just wide. Shortly after, slack defending by Darlington let Kidderminster's Hemmings win possession on the edge of the box, but five defenders quickly got back to cover; in addition, his shot lacked power and was easily saved by Connell. It was very nearly 2-0 after 80 minutes when Thompson got into the box on the right and crossed to the far post, where Justin Donawa's header hit a defender a couple of yards out and was saved. Connell pulled off a superb one-handed save on 89 minutes. A cross came over from the right, substitute Ollie Shenton came steaming in at the far post and his effort was going into the top-right corner, until the stopper somehow managed to claw the ball away and over the bar with an outstretched left arm to the loud cheers of the fans. This ensured that three points remained in possession of the home side when the final whistle went.

As Chris and I waited for our taxi in the bar, we bumped into John Gray. The pair of us agreed that Jarrett Rivers had been excellent throughout the whole of the game and was proving to have been a very good signing by manager Alun Armstrong.

One final comment on Jarrett: ever since he signed for the club, he's been one of my favourite players of the post-2012 era. Every year, I sponsor his home shirt and I'm very proud to do so.

* * *

Will Hatfield – Career Details

Will Hatfield came through the Leeds United youth system, having joined the club as an eight-year-old. His first matchday involvement for the first team came on 3 February 2010 as an unused substitute in a 3-1 home defeat to Tottenham Hotspur in an FA Cup fourth-round replay. He joined Conference Premier side York City on 28 January 2011 on a one-month loan and played four matches.

The midfielder signed for League Two club Accrington Stanley on 14 October 2011 on a month's loan. He made his debut the following day as a half-time substitute in a 2-0 home defeat to Swindon Town. Having made four appearances, his loan was extended until the end of December 2011.

Will left Leeds on 12 January 2012 after agreeing to mutually terminate his contract. He signed for FC Halifax Town later that month, making his debut on 24 January 2012 as a 66th-minute substitute in a 2-2 home draw with Gainsborough Trinity in Conference North.

On 10 February 2012, Hatfield re-signed for Accrington Stanley on a contract until the end of 2011/12 season, then penned a new one-year deal in June 2012. He once scored four goals in an FA Cup tie against AFC Fylde on 3 November 2012.

Hatfield rejoined Halifax on 27 November 2014 on a 28-day loan and joined the Conference Premier club permanently on 15 January 2015 after leaving his parent club by mutual consent. When his contract expired, he signed for newly promoted Guiseley on 19 June 2015, in what was now known as the National League, and went on to spend four seasons with them. He left in July 2019 and signed for National League North club Darlington.

Will was named as Darlington's away player of the year, players' player of the year and player of the year for 2019/20, as well as winning their goal of the season award for his strike against Kidderminster Harriers.

On 22 March 2022, Hatfield signed for fellow National League North club AFC Fylde for an undisclosed fee.

At the time of writing he is still with Fylde, back in the National League.

My Memorable Match Involving Will Hatfield

Walsall v Darlington, FA Cup first round – 2019/20

Due to my continuing health problems, after much discussion, we decided to get a taxi from Darlington to Walsall the day before the game and then come back the day after. This may seem a crazy, extravagant way to go to a football match that's well over 100 miles away but, given my needs, it was definitely the best option.

Anyway, prior to leaving, the three of us decided to book a meal in Walsall's excellent hospitality suite. We weren't to be disappointed as it turned out to be really good value for money.

I have to say, the suite afforded a brilliant view of the pitch so we decided to watch the match from inside, given that it was a cold day.

The three of us witnessed an excellent performance from Darlington, who were playing against a team that were not only full-time (Darlington since their relegation to the Northern League in 2012 were part-time) but also two leagues above them.

As early as the 17th minute, Darlington were a goal up with Jamaican international Omar Holness scoring from the rebound after what was a brilliant save from Walsall keeper Jack Rose when he parried an original shot from the same player. The Quakers managed to hold on to their lead until the interval.

The hosts came more into the game in the second period and it came as no surprise when Caolan Lavery poked the ball home in the 86th minute. Worse was to follow when three minutes later the home side took the lead after the disappointing Darlington keeper Liam Connell punched the ball into his own net following a corner. Connell had also been at fault for the first goal when he had failed to hold on to the original shot prior to Lavery scoring. Darlington poured men forward following Walsall's second goal and were rewarded seven minutes into injury time when former Middlesbrough midfielder Joe Wheatley bundled the ball home following a free kick from the now sadly deceased Osagi Bascome. This sent the hundreds of visiting supporters wild and gave Darlo a richly deserved replay.

Incidentally, both teams finished the game with ten men after Dan Scarr for Walsall and Darlington's Ben Hedley were sent off.

One thing I noticed was Will Hatfield's work rate in this match. He must have covered every blade of grass, in what was an excellent midfield performance.

Unfortunately, Darlington lost the replay 1-0 at Blackwell Meadows, a game that was featured on BT Sport. I went with Chris, but I had to leave at half-time due to the extreme cold.

4

Strikers

Colin Sinclair – Career Details

Colin Sinclair played in the Scottish Football League for Raith Rovers and Dunfermline Athletic as well as in the English Football League for Darlington, Hereford United and Newport County. A forward, he made more than 300 appearances in all and ended his career where it had started, with Scottish junior club Linlithgow Rose.

The popular striker was a member of the Darlington 'Dream Team' selected in 2003 via a competition in the club's match programme, as part of the 'Farewell to Feethams' celebrations when the club left its longtime home ground.

After retiring from football he went on to develop a successful career in both the licensed and hotel trades from his base in Linlithgow.

My Memorable Match Involving Colin Sinclair

Darlington v Swansea City – 1974/75

My mother took me to see this, the first game of the 1974/75 season. We witnessed a feisty opening to the game with the visitors making all the early running. It came as no surprise when they opened the scoring in the tenth minute as Dave Roberts found himself in space down the right wing and his measured cross was side-footed home by Peter Abbott. They continued to dominate the first half with Darlington unable to

151

cope with their tough tackling and physical approach. Fouls littered the match, which spoiled the event as a spectacle.

At half-time I can remember being really disappointed with Darlington's first-half performance. After all, I'd waited all summer for the new season to start and my beloved team had stuttered all the way through the first 45 minutes. I was frustrated to say the least.

However, I needn't have worried as a few choice words must have been said by the manager Billy Horner during the break. He certainly got the response that he was looking for and it took only four minutes of the second half for the Quakers to draw level. Good work down the right by Colin Sinclair led to a cross into the box and a smart finish from debutant striker Stan Webb.

The home side were on top and the game swung further their way on 56 minutes when visiting full-back Stephen Thomas was sent off for throwing a punch at Sinclair. The ten men struggled to cope with the strong running of the Darlington front three of Don Burluraux, Sinclair and Webb and wilted in the heat as the hosts took complete control. Darlington went ahead on 70 minutes when Burluraux created space and fired towards goal. Derek Bellotti, who had played so well in the City goal, seemed to have the shot covered, but the ball took a wicked deflection off Pat Lally that wrong-footed the keeper and rolled into the net. It was 3-1 on 87 minutes when Burluraux opened up the visitors' defence and Webb met his cross at the far post and smashed the ball into the roof of the net for his second goal of the afternoon. Swansea pulled a goal back with the last kick of the game when Dave Bruton fired home from the edge of the box after a Geoff Thomas free kick, but it was too little too late for the Welshmen as Darlington easily held on and took the two points.

As I sat in my bedroom, I can remember thinking that Colin Sinclair had changed the game when he had crossed for Stan Webb to equalise. That set Darlington on their way to the victory.

I always liked Colin and was gutted when he was sold to Hereford United a few years later.

* * *

Stan Webb – Career Details

Stan Webb scored 40 goals in 167 appearances in the Football League for Middlesbrough, Carlisle United, Brentford and Darlington in the 1970s.

A forward, he also played non-league football for several clubs including Whitby Town and Guisborough Town, for whom he scored the club's first FA Cup goal, in the 1978/79 first qualifying round against Consett.

My Memorable Match Involving Stan Webb

Darlington v Swansea City – 1975/76

I attended with my mother. Despite it being midweek, once again I skived school, simply because Darlington needed a point to avoid re-election and I didn't want to miss the match.

Stan Webb scored for the home team in the 65th minute and Swansea equalised in the 85th through Alan Curtis.

The celebrations after the final whistle were unbelievable; the players were dancing on the pitch and the fans were singing, 'We are the champions'. The club had achieved their aim of not finishing in the bottom four and therefore not having to apply for re-election. That sadly was the limit of their ambition at that particular time.

Nowadays, a manager would be sacked if his team finished fifth from bottom of the table. How times change!

Apart from the celebrations, which looking back now, were crazy, I can remember being super excited when Stan Webb blasted the ball home to give the Quakers the lead. Over time, that stayed in my memory, rather than what happened after the final whistle.

* * *

Ron Ferguson – Career Details

Ron Ferguson was born in Accrington, Lancashire. He began his career as a youngster with Sheffield Wednesday and made his first team debut on 9 November 1974, a couple of months after his 17th birthday. He scored the opening goal in a 3-0 defeat of York City in the Second Division and finished the season with 11 appearances. In December 1975, Ron joined Fourth Division club Scunthorpe United on loan; he played three times without scoring. His parent club released him in the second half of the 1975/76 season and he signed for Fourth Division Darlington, for whom he scored the only goal of the game against Torquay United on 15 March 1976.

In just over four seasons with Darlington, he made 114 league appearances and scored 18 goals.

In 1980, Ron began a six-season spell with Racing Jet de Bruxelles, then of the Belgian Second Division. During that time they were relegated to the third tier. He then enjoyed two successive promotions to spend the 1984/85 season in the First Division, but unfortunately they were relegated. However, they were promoted in 1986, but that year Ron moved on to La Louvière, where he spent three seasons playing in the third tier.

My Memorable Match Involving Ron Ferguson

Darlington v Sheffield Wednesday, FA Cup second round – 1976/77

I went to this match with my mother where we witnessed one of the best goals ever scored at Feethams.

From what I can remember, the game was an ill-tempered affair and the start of the second half was even delayed for eight minutes after fighting broke out on the pitch between the rival sets of fans. With only minutes remaining, 19-year-old Ron Ferguson picked up the ball and raced towards the Tin Shed. This is his account of what happened next:

'I remember going past one player and then heard Eddie Rowles shout from some distance, "For Christ's sake hit it, and hit it well, we're all knackered." That's what I did, but I wasn't far from the bench, and I heard them shout, "What's he doing? ... For crying out loud ... he hasn't has he?" Then I remember time standing still.'

What Ferguson had actually done was to unleash a blistering shot from all of 35 yards which dipped over the Wednesday keeper Chris Turner and into the top corner of the net. It was one of those archetypal Ronnie Radford goals.

What made this even more special for Ron was that the Owls had released him a few months previously, and I can recall him going over to the dugout after he had scored the winning goal and sticking two fingers up to Len Ashurst, the Wednesday manager at the time! I liked Ferguson after that. He was a big centre-forward who used to go in really hard. He was my kind of player!

I couldn't get over Ron's goal and I went on and on about it while my mother pushed me home. I bet that she was sick of hearing about it by the time we reached our front door!

* * *

Eddie Rowles – Career Details

Eddie Rowles started his career with Bournemouth & Boscombe Athletic in March 1968. He joined York City in July 1971 and was their top scorer for the 1972/73 season, with nine goals.

Eddie signed for Torquay United in June 1973 and once again, he was their top scorer in his first season.

He then moved to Darlington in August 1975 and was their leading scorer in the 1976/77 season and was a crowd favourite. Eddie left the Quakers to join Colchester United in December 1977; he stayed there until 1982, when he retired from football.

My Memorable Match Involving Eddie Rowles
Darlington v Wimbledon 1977/78

I went to see the above game with my mother. We saw Darlington very nearly take the lead after only two minutes when Ron Ferguson cut in from the right and drove a low cross-come-shot into the goalmouth. Dons defender Dave Donaldson deflected the ball and it seemed to be sneaking just inside the far post before keeper Dick Teale launched himself full length and clawed it wide. The game then developed into a scrappy, hard-fought stalemate with chances at a premium.

The stalemate was eventually broken after 30 minutes with a spectacular strike by Darlington central defender Neil Hague. Barry Lyons intercepted a clearance and made progress down the right. His cross into the box was headed wide by Dons centre-half Billy Edwards. From the resultant corner Jimmy Seal headed towards goal but it was hacked clear by full-back Dave Galvin. The clearance fell perfectly for Hague who smashed a left-footed volley into the top corner from fully 30 yards out with Teale absolutely helpless. Wimbledon scored a shock equaliser a minute before half-time when the ball bounced awkwardly in the Quakers area and referee Mike Peck ruled that John Stone had handled. Billy Holmes stepped up to send Phil Owers the wrong way from the spot.

The second half began with the home side on top and they nearly regained the lead when Eddie Rowles broke clear down the right and squared the ball into the middle where Lyons volleyed just over. The Quakers were back in front after 58 minutes. Full-back Jimmy Cochrane played a short free kick to Stone whose deep cross to the far post was missed by Steve Galliers but met by Clive Nattress. He completely miss-hit his shot from an acute angle but the ball bobbled across the goalmouth and into the net just inside the far post.

The visitors tried to respond and went close to an equaliser when Owers misjudged a left-wing corner, but Derek Craig was on hand to head the ball out for another corner from under his own crossbar. Darlington made the game safe in the 81st minute with another controversial penalty decision. Ferguson went down just inside the box after an innocuous-looking challenge by Edwards. Referee Peck thought it worthy of a penalty and Dennis Wann sent Teale the wrong way from the spot.

As my mother pushed me home, I thought about the game. I was watching certain players and Eddie Rowles caught my eye that day. His unselfish running off the ball was impressive. This stuck in my mind, as it was the first time I'd done this.

* * *

John Stalker – Career Details

John Stalker began his senior career in England with Leicester City, but moved on to Darlington in 1979. He scored 36 goals from 116 appearances in the Football League. After a short spell with Hartlepool United, the striker returned to his native Scotland, where he played in the Scottish League for Meadowbank Thistle and East Fife before moving into junior football with Penicuik Athletic and Newtongrange Star.

My Memorable Match Involving John Stalker

Darlington v Northampton Town – 1980/81

By 1980, I was 15 and could communicate much better, so my mother decided to take me to the games, leave me there, do her shopping, and then come back for me, something she did for this particular game for the very first time.

Only goalkeeper Pat Cuff and midfielder Harry Charlton were over the age of 24 in a very young, inexperienced side that started this match. It was captained by Donald Ball, who at 18 was the youngest skipper in the Football League.

In the Feethams sunshine, Darlington won 1-0 with a John Stalker goal just before half-time, in front of 1,763 fans.

It was a poor match, mostly fought in the midfield. The only thing of any worth to come out of the game was Stalker's strike. He hit the ball from just inside the box, giving the visiting keeper no chance.

As I sat at home reading my programme, I got to thinking that John Stalker and Alan Walsh could end up being a potent strike force. Little did I know that by May 1981, they would have scored 40 goals between them!

* * *

Alan Walsh – Career Details

Alan Walsh began his career in 1977 with Middlesbrough, but moved to Darlington the following year. He spent six years at the club, where he became their record scorer with 87 goals in the league and 100 overall.

In 1984 Alan joined Bristol City, where he amassed 218 Football League appearances, winning their player of the season award in 1987/88. During his time with the Robins, he became renowned as an early exponent of the step over football skill, colloquially known as the 'Walshy shuffle', later to be popularised by players such as Cristiano Ronaldo. In 1986, the striker collected a winners' medal as part of the Bristol City team that beat Bolton Wanderers 3-0 in the Football League Trophy Final.

He moved to Turkish club Beşiktaş in 1989, where he won two Süper Lig titles, before finishing his professional career back in England with short spells at Walsall, Huddersfield Town, Shrewsbury Town, Southampton, Hartlepool United and Cardiff City.

After retiring from playing he rejoined Bristol City as a coach and stayed with the club for 11 years in a variety of coaching roles, lastly as development coach, a position he left on 19 October 2011. He joined Bristol Rovers as youth team coach in 2012, a role he held until 2016. Later, Alan did some scouting for Stoke City but this ceased when the COVID-19 pandemic started in 2020.

One final comment regarding Alan: I've known him since 1980 and over the years we have occasionally kept in touch, more so recently. During these conversations, being the nosey person I am, I've asked him quite a few questions regarding his career. Firstly why did he leave Middlesbrough to sign for Darlington in 1978/79? This was his reply in his own words, 'I had been at Middlesbrough for nearly two seasons and for the majority of that time I was playing regularly in the reserves. Joining Darlington was an opportunity to play first-team football.' I also queried if he regretted leaving Darlington just before

1984/85. His answer was interesting, 'I was very disappointed to leave Darlington. Cyril [Knowles] was building a good squad to challenge for promotion which proved to be the successful outcome at the end of the season. In football you have to make difficult decisions and we – that is my wife Sue and I – made the decision to move to Bristol City to progress my future career.'

These are just a couple of examples of conversations I've had with Alan. I regard him as a friend and long may this continue.

My Memorable Match Involving Alan Walsh
Darlington v Hartlepool United 1981/82

My mother dropped me off at Feethams for this match against our local rivals. As per the norm, I took my place in the East Stand Paddock.

Unfortunately, Darlington made a disastrous start, conceding two sloppy goals in the first 17 minutes. Firstly, keeper Pat Cuff made a mess of a John Linacre cross and Darlington old boy Alan Harding scored at the second attempt, after his first effort was blocked by Kevan Smith. Minutes later, Cuff misjudged another cross from Linacre and Harry Clarke headed home to put the visitors 2-0 up. Darlington were stung into action and dominated the rest of the first half, but were kept out by another ex-Quaker, goalkeeper Martin Burleigh, who made a string of fine saves, as Smith, David Speedie and Roger Wicks all went close. When the keeper was beaten, he was helped out by his defenders, as Harding and John Bird both made goal-line clearances. The visitors finally cracked in the 40th minute when Wicks curled in a free kick that was headed home by Dave McLean to make the half-time score 2-1.

The second half became the 'Alan Walsh Show'. Playing against his hometown club, he terrorised the visitors' defence with a brilliant individual display. A minute after the restart, he cut in from the right and unleashed an unstoppable drive into the top corner from 25 yards out for the equaliser – Walsh later claimed it to be the best goal he'd ever scored. Fellow striker Tony McFadden then shot just over the bar as the home side applied more pressure. The turning point of the game came in the 67th minute when David Linighan handled a Speedie pass and gave away a penalty. Walsh blazed over the bar, but scored at the second attempt when the referee ordered the kick to be retaken because of encroachment. The striker then completed his 23-minute hat-trick with another long-range effort two minutes later, driving home a Dave Hawker pass and scored his fourth of the night in the last minute when heading home a Speedie cross. From being 2-0 down after 17 minutes, Darlington had come back to win 5-2 in what was an enthralling match.

As my mother pushed me home, I couldn't get over how good Alan Walsh had been in the second half. He'd completely taken Hartlepool apart in a performance that I'll never forget.

* * *

David Speedie – Career Details

Born in Glenrothes in Scotland, but raised in Yorkshire, David Speedie worked as a coal miner and played for Brodsworth Welfare before signing professional terms with Barnsley in 1978. After 21 appearances he moved to Darlington in 1980, where his talent first became apparent. Just two years later, he was spotted by the then Chelsea manager John Neal, who signed him for £65,000 in May 1982.

David had a five-year stint at Chelsea where he formed a prolific strike partnership with Kerry Dixon. Speedie's strength, scoring prowess, work rate and unlikely heading ability (he is 5ft 7in tall) perfectly complemented Dixon and winger Pat Nevin as the trio notched up almost 200 goals between them in three years. Before the arrival of Nevin and Dixon, however, David had played an important part in Chelsea's survival in the Second Division a year earlier, with his seven goals (including two on his debut against Oldham Athletic) that season proving crucial. He was Chelsea's player of the year in 1985 and popular with the fans for his consistent, gutsy performances.

In 1986, he became the first senior player since Geoff Hurst in the 1966 World Cup Final to score three goals at Wembley, as Chelsea defeated Manchester City 5-4 in the Full Members' Cup Final, after they had led 5-1. That year Chelsea finished sixth in the league, having been in the hunt for the title for most of the season before a late slump in form ruled them out of contention in the final weeks.

Speedie left Chelsea in 1987 with three years left on his contract due to disagreements with the hierarchy. Having scored 64 goals in 205 appearances for the west London side, he joined Coventry City for £750,000 in July 1987. His first appearance was in the 1987 FA Charity Shield against Everton where he narrowly missed out on scoring on his debut. This statistic would be rectified just a week later, however, when in an effective replay of the 1987 FA Cup Final at Highfield Road, he scored with a fine low shot past Ray Clemence to set up a 2-1 win over Spurs. While Coventry were hampered in their post-cup final season by a disintegrating pitch, David earned the notable distinction of scoring a hat-trick while finishing on the losing side in a 4-3 defeat against Middlesbrough.

He combined with the aerial strength of Cyrille Regis and the wide options of David Smith, David Phillips, Micky Gynn and Brian Borrows to score some memorable goals. In 1989 his chipped winner at high-flying Norwich City, a week after an FA Cup defeat to non-league Sutton United, was almost universally described in the press as 'sublime'. This became the Speedie trademark at Coventry and was used to great effect against the likes of Wimbledon and Southampton. He was a key component in the Coventry team in the 1988/89 campaign, beating champions elect Arsenal and riding as high as third in the league as late as February. They would only lose five games on their travels that season, winning the same number away from home. Their seventh-placed finish was only the third time they had achieved a position inside the top eight.

The latter half of his spell at Coventry would see him drop back into a deeper midfield role which led to a significant reduction in his goals tally. He enjoyed a period of just under four years at Highfield Road, none of which were relegation battles, scoring 35 goals in all competitions. This was the same as his Chelsea strike rate and enabled him to maintain a presence in the Scotland side. David left the Sky Blues amid the turbulent and transitional autumn/ winter period of 1990/91, which would see manager John Sillett replaced by Terry Butcher.

David joined Liverpool in January 1991 and became Kenny Dalglish's last signing before his resignation the following month. Dalglish had been interested in signing Speedie four years earlier when he was still at Chelsea.

He scored on his Liverpool debut at Old Trafford, then netted twice in the Merseyside derby in the next league game, and by the end of the season he had scored six goals for the Reds – all in the league.

However, his Liverpool career was cut short when Graeme Souness took over as manager and he was sold that summer to Blackburn Rovers, where Dalglish returned to management soon afterwards. On the final day of the 1991/92 season, Speedie scored three goals in a win which relegated Plymouth Argyle but most significantly fired Rovers into the play-offs and would be a major step towards a new era for the club, beginning with a play-off final victory which took them into the new Premier League, which they won three years later.

Unfortunately, David was not to be part of Blackburn's Premier League adventures. He was sold to Southampton for £400,000, replacing Alan Shearer who moved the other way for £3.6m, a then national record fee. He joined the Saints at the same time as his old Chelsea strike partner Kerry Dixon.

Speedie made just 11 appearances, without scoring, for Southampton in 1992/93, making his Premier League debut in August 1992. He then had unsuccessful loan spells with Birmingham City and West Bromwich Albion before another loan deal in early March took him to First Division promotion contenders West Ham United. His four goals in 11 league games helped the Hammers secure automatic promotion to the Premier League as runners-up.

David was not offered a permanent contract with West Ham. Instead, he accepted an offer from Brian Little to sign for First Division promotion hopefuls Leicester City. He scored 12 goals in 37 league games for the East Midlands side in 1993/94 as they qualified for the play-offs and sealed promotion to the Premier League by defeating local rivals Derby County 2-1 in the final at Wembley. He was injured for that game and retired later in the year due to injury, having never featured in the Premier League for the Foxes.

The striker made his senior debut for Scotland on 25 May 1985 in a 1-0 Rous Cup win over England. He won the last of his ten full caps on 30 May 1989 against Chile, also a Rous Cup tie, which Scotland won 2-0. However, he never scored an international goal.

David continued his career at non-league level for a host of clubs including Stamford AFC and Hendon where he made five appearances while failing to score. Indeed, his most impressive 45 minutes came as a replacement goalkeeper for the second half of Hendon's first game of 1996/97 against Sutton United after first choice Scott Ashcroft was injured just before half-time. He also made a handful of Northern League appearances for Crook Town. He retired having scored 150 career goals.

Speedie lived for a while in Dublin where he commentated on Setanta Sports and played for Francis AFC in Dublin's United Churches League.

My Memorable Match Involving David Speedie
Darlington v Southampton – 1981/82

In 1982, there was yet another financial crisis at Darlington. The Quakers had experienced many such problems during their 99-year history. This one was so severe that it threatened the very existence of the football club. At the AGM in November, record losses of £48,000 were reported from the previous season, bringing the total debt to £74,000. It was also revealed that the club were losing over £800 per week, but chairman Leslie Moore insisted that there was no cash crisis. Things became considerably worse in December and January, however, when bad weather took hold. Three consecutive home games were postponed which meant that no money was coming in through the turnstiles. The problem reached crisis point at the end of January, when a special press conference was called at Feethams and Moore announced that if £50,000 wasn't raised within the next six weeks the club would fold. They were now £95,000 in debt and had zero cash available to pay any of their bills, including the weekly wage bill of £4,000.

As often happens in situations like that the football community rallied round with offers of help. South Shields were the first club to chip in with a cheque for £100. Sunderland were next on the phone, offering to send their first team for a money-raising friendly. They visited Feethams on 2 March and a crowd of 5,518 paid receipts of £5,400. The attendance figure included the Sunderland players, who manager Alan Durban insisted paid to get in through the turnstiles!

Southampton, managed by Lawrie McMenemy, also promised to play at Feethams to raise much-needed funds. The Saints were riding high in the top flight at the time. They'd spent six weeks on top of the table throughout January and February but by the time of this match they had dropped down to fifth. Their team was packed with big-name players and internationals such as Kevin Keegan, Alan Ball, Mick Channon, Chris Nicholl and ex-Middlesbrough star David Armstrong. With this in mind, they would provide quite an attraction and draw a large crowd. To play this match was a magnificent gesture by McMenemy and his club.

The Saints visited Feethams on Sunday, 18 April. They'd travelled north to play at Leeds on the Saturday, winning 3-1, and stayed in the region to play at Darlington the following day. The Quakers had enjoyed a 3-0 home win over Northampton on the Saturday and so had the curious distinction of entertaining Northampton and Southampton on consecutive days.

I went to this match with my mother. She stayed with me on this occasion because she wanted to see Kevin Keegan play in the flesh. The pair of us were lucky enough to see an absolutely brilliant game of football.

The visitors showed their First Division class early on and controlled the opening stages. They took the lead on 27 minutes when a cheeky back-heel by Keegan gave Dave Puckett a clear run on goal and he comfortably slotted the ball past Pat Cuff. They increased their lead eight minutes later when a clever jinking run down the left by David Armstrong took him to the byline from where he crossed for Mick Channon to head home. Minutes later, Armstrong shaved the post as Southampton threatened to run riot, but the Quakers got back into the game just before half-time. From a Tony McFadden through ball, David Speedie advanced into the box, held off Nick Holmes and fired past Ivan Katalinić in the Saints' goal.

Darlington began the second half in fine style and took complete control of the game. Defender Peter Skipper headed wide on 57 minutes when well placed and minutes later so did Ian Hamilton. In between their efforts, from a rare attack by the visitors, Channon fired wide, before Alan Walsh hit one of his trademark screamers just wide of the mark. The deserved equaliser came in the 51st minute when a Walsh cross into the box was met by Speedie who spectacularly volleyed home. Two minutes later the Quakers were in front as striker Tony McFadden raced through a static defence and slotted past Katalinić. The same player almost scored again but fired his shot into the side netting and at the other end Mark Wright headed against the post as the entertainment continued.

Speedie completed his hat-trick in the 66th minute. Dave McLean took a quick free kick and the Scot reacted quickest to head home. A minute later he almost made it four for the afternoon but his shot hit the keeper. Ten minutes from time Mark Wright brought down Walsh in the area and referee George Courtney had no hesitation in pointing to the spot. Walsh fired home the penalty to make the final score 5-2.

After this match I knew for certain that David Speedie wouldn't be a Darlington player the following season. He was simply unplayable in the second half and was clearly good enough to play at a far higher level.

I was spot on as David signed for Chelsea for £65,000, but not before giving me his prized number six Darlington shirt. It remains one of my most treasured possessions to this day, over 40 years later.

* * *

John Hannah – Career Details

John Hannah played in the Football League as a forward for Darlington. He also played non-league football for Fryston Colliery Welfare and Scarborough.

John, who had been working as an electrician at Kellingley Colliery, joined the Quakers on a non-contract basis, and played for them during the 1984 miners' strike.

My Memory of John Hannah

Once again, my main memory of John Hannah didn't occur on the football pitch. Let me explain.

I was on the train going to Bristol to see Bristol City v Darlington and found myself sat next to the then club captain, Dave McLean.

When Dave suggested playing a game of cards, John came to join us in order to make a foursome with Tom, the guy I was with – not his real name – and me.

To my surprise, we ended up playing my favourite game, three card brag, and I ended up winning handsomely. In our final hand, the stake crept up inexorably from 50p, to £1, to £5 and then to £10 until I mischievously increased it to £50.

By this time the pot contained well over £200 and John would have needed £50 just to see me, so he threw in his strong hand of three queens. My bluff had worked. When he saw me scooping up the pot with my miserable hand of ten high he quite understandably exclaimed, 'You bastard!'

Anyway, I felt guilty about taking so much money from him, especially as he was still on strike, so I gave him a sizeable chunk of the money back and he thanked me for being a gentleman.

Unfortunately, I never got to know John that well. However, on the few occasions I met him, he was always reminded of that card game.

I liked him and thought that he did an excellent job for the team at that particular time.

* * *

Carl Airey – Career Details

Carl Airey was a bustling striker, who began his career as an apprentice with Barnsley, turning professional in February 1983 and making his league debut the same season. He also spent a period on loan at Bradford City where he failed to score in five games at the start of the 1983/84 season. He left Oakwell in August 1984, after 38 league games in which he scored five goals, and joined Darlington. Carl was top scorer the following season as the Quakers, under Cyril Knowles, won promotion to the Third Division. He went on to score 28 goals in 75 league games.

Carl was transferred to Belgian side Charleroi in May 1986. His stay was short-lived and he only made three appearances without scoring. He returned to England in December of the same year for a loan to Chesterfield, playing 26 league games and scoring four goals.

In August 1987 Airey was on the move once more, this time to Rotherham United, scoring 11 goals in 32 league games. He teamed up again with Knowles and former team-mate Phil Lloyd when he joined Torquay United in December 1988. He made his debut on 20 January 1989 when he came on as a substitute for Ian Weston in a 2-0 defeat away to Halifax Town. He struggled to establish himself in the starting 11, although he did start at Wembley in the 1989 Associate Members' Cup Final against Bolton Wanderers.

The following season, he started as first choice, but soon lost his place and along with Weston joined Shamrock Rovers on loan in September 1989 where after five appearances, he returned to the Torquay side the following month and equalled Sammy Collins's record of scoring in seven consecutive games before losing his place again and not featuring again in the first team after the end of January. He was released at the end of the season and joined Salisbury in July 1990.

I met up with Carl in the early 1990s when Darlington played at Torquay. He told me that he was working as a milkman in Salisbury and had retired from football.

My Memorable Match Involving Carl Airey
Torquay United v Darlington – 1984/85

Only four Darlington fans in a Ford Capri made the 350-mile journey to Torquay in September 1984, and I am proud to say I was one of them. To make matters worse, the match was an evening kick-off so we had to set off at about ten in the morning. I travelled with a lad called Gavin and two other Darlo fans, whose names escape me with the passing of time.

Stopping twice at service stations en route, we arrived in Torquay at about five o'clock and after some fish and chips to line our stomachs, we also had a few pints in a pub near the ground.

Prior to the kick-off, it quickly became apparent that Steve Tupling and former Scottish international Willie Young were making their debuts for the Quakers.

On to the game itself, and although we forced 14 corners to the home side's five, that was a misleading statistic since the Gulls hit the post twice and scored in the tenth minute. By contrast, Darlington played very poorly and were lucky to be only 1-0 down at the break.

Torquay were so much the better side that I do believe if it had been a boxing match the referee would have intervened and stopped it. But the Quakers hung on gamely and got a corner with three minutes remaining, which was taken by

Dave McLean. The ball was flicked on at the near post by midfielder Colin Ross and Carl Airey gleefully headed in the equaliser.

All I can remember is going absolutely mental, celebrating the goal, as the Torquay supporters were predictably singing, 'You're going to get your f****ng heads kicked in!' I think they must have been quite upset, because two policemen had to escort the four of us back to our car for our own safety.

The following day, I spoke with Ian about the match. I told him that Carl Airey was the difference for Darlington. Despite the team not playing well, he battled on gamely and deserved his goal. Such performances became the norm for him, but this was the first time I'd seen it. That's why it stuck in my mind.

* * *

John McMahon – Career Details

John McMahon played as a forward in the Football League on a non-contract basis for Darlington. He was previously an apprentice with Middlesbrough and also played non-league football for Guisborough Town.

McMahon joined Darlington in March 1985 and made four substitute appearances without scoring as the club gained promotion from the Fourth Division. He also started three Associate Members' Cup matches and scored three goals.

Sadly, John passed away in late 2023.

My Memorable Match Involving John McMahon

Darlington v Halifax Town, Associate Members' Cup first round second leg – 1984/85

I went with Stephen Lowson. I have to say, the pair of us witnessed a really good game of football.

It took John McMahon only five minutes of his debut to open his account as a Darlington player with a deft finish. He scored his second on 23 minutes with a clever flicked header from full-back Graeme Aldred's cross. The Quakers were completely on top and playing some of their best football of the season and scored their third goal on 36 minutes when Steve Tupling turned and fired home after good work by left-back Mike Sanderson. A minute later, McMahon slotted home to complete his hat-trick and give the home side the aggregate lead having lost the first leg 4-1 at The Shay – a game that I'd also witnessed.

Darlington continued to dominate the second half and Tupling thought he'd added to the lead when he netted in the 63rd minute, but the whistle had already gone for a handball by a Halifax defender in the box and Dave McLean fired home the penalty. The game continued in a completely one-sided fashion and McLean scored his second of the afternoon on 72 minutes with a superb long-range strike, and Tupling added the seventh goal five minutes from time.

The 7-0 victory meant that Darlington won the overall tie 8-4 and were drawn at home to Lincoln City in the second round.

As Stephen pushed me home, I thought that John McMahon would be a good signing. Unfortunately, he wasn't really given a run in the team because Carl Airey and Garry MacDonald were really good throughout that season. However, I never forgot that first-half three-goal blast.

* * *

Mark Forster – Career Details

Mark Forster started his career at Middlesbrough before moving on to Leicester City. He signed for Darlington during the 1983/84 season.

Mark scored 13 goals from 38 appearances in the Football League for Darlington and contributed to their promotion to the Third Division in 1985.

After retiring through injury in 1986, Mark went on to play non-league football for clubs including Guisborough Town (where he also managed) and South Bank.

At the time of writing, Mark works in the financial sector.

My Memories of Mark Forster

Over the years, Mark Forster has become a very good friend of mine, so as with a few other players in this book my main memories of him are not match-related, even though I have to say that he was a very good player.

Three things regarding Mark stick in my mind, so here goes.

Shortly before kick-off, Mark promised to throw me his shirt after the promotion-clinching game at Crewe Alexandra in 1984/85. Anyway, I caught it, but some moron wrenched it out of my hand and within a few seconds, it was gone for ever. I can remember being gutted at the time. Some 14 years later, I bumped into Mark at a Darlington FC reunion. In the course of our conversation, I happened to mention this incident. When he heard my tale, he promised to give me a signed shirt from the promotion-winning season. True to his word, he posted the shirt through my letterbox the following day. At the time, I thought, 'What a lovely gesture.' From that day on we became firm friends, and have remained so ever since.

Mark also wrote the foreword for my book *Give Them Wings*, which was published in April 2021, for which I was eternally grateful.

In between writing the foreword, Mark came to celebrate the marriage between Jen and I. He made a lovely speech and I can honestly say, I'm proud to have him as a friend.

As well as these three memories one other story springs to mind. Here are the details in Mark's own words:

'One afternoon, Paul and I went for a lunchtime drink at a pub near to where he used to work in Birtley. As we approached the entrance, I noticed the four or five steps that led into the bar and wondered how we would cope. Paul told me not to worry and to turn his wheelchair around and pull him up the steps, just as you would do with a pram or a pushchair. Task easily accomplished, I thought, as we settled down to our drinks and sandwiches. Pushing a wheelchair didn't seem to be so hard after all!

'However, leaving the bar taught me otherwise! Paul asked me to push him down forwards while keeping the weight of his body balanced against me. No problem I thought, until I found myself, only two steps down, hanging on to a wheelchair at 45 degrees, with the occupant holding on for dear life!

'I eventually managed to get the chair and Paul down in one piece and took several deep breaths after being very close to suffering a hernia. It was only when I noticed him lying in a crumpled heap in the chair that I realised the job was by no means complete.'

I have never forgotten that incident and the two of us still laugh about it to this day!

* * *

Garry MacDonald – Career Details

Garry MacDonald began his career with Middlesbrough and made his first-team debut for them on 8 November 1980, aged 18, in the starting 11 for a 1-0 win away to Brighton & Hove Albion in the First Division. He made 16 appearances in his first two seasons, at the end of which Middlesbrough were relegated to the Second Division. He went on to make 61 appearances before being released in 1984.

Garry began the 1984/85 season with another Second Division club, Carlisle United, before moving on in October to Darlington of the Fourth Division under the management of Cyril Knowles. He made 33 league appearances as the team gained promotion to the Third Division. In addition, he played in all six of their FA Cup ties and scored in the third round replay, covered earlier in this book, as Darlington eliminated Middlesbrough 2-1. Some 20 years later, that match was voted the best ever played at the Feethams ground.

The striker top scored for Darlington in 1985/86 with 16 league goals but injury deprived him of the chance to partner new signing David Currie the following season, at the end of which they were relegated. In 1987/88, Garry played regularly alongside Currie, whose performances earned him a move to a higher level. MacDonald, however, stayed with Darlington for one more season, but left when they were relegated out of the Football League into the Conference. During his time with the Quakers he scored 47 goals from 196 appearances in all competitions.

After a few months with Stockport County, during which he made only four first-team appearances, Cyril Knowles signed him again, this time for Hartlepool United in December 1989 for a £5,000 fee. Garry made 16 appearances that season but scored only once and after three more matches, in the 1990/91 season, he moved into non-league football with South Bank.

My Memorable Match Involving Garry MacDonald
Exeter City v Darlington – 1984/85

I went to this match with Tom on the train – a seven-hour journey.

When we arrived at Exeter, Tom informed me that he wanted to look around the cathedral, which fortunately, or unfortunately whichever way you look at it, was only a short distance from the station. I must admit that going on an impromptu sightseeing tour was hardly at the top of my list of priorities! To be truthful, as he pushed me through the nave I was like Andy from the TV comedy *Little Britain*, bored out of my mind and gagging for a drink!

Anyway, back to the real purpose behind our mammoth train journey. The game itself was certainly an eventful affair. Our goalkeeper, Fred Barber, saved a seventh-minute penalty. Then our debutant Garry MacDonald scored with a tame shot from the edge of the area in the 34th minute. Exeter, though, equalised with seven minutes remaining on the clock.

During the long journey home, while I read my programme, I thought that overall, it had been a good performance from Darlington and that Garry MacDonald looked to have been a great signing. My assumption proved to be right, as he scored a lot of crucial goals that season.

* * *

Dale Anderson – Career Details

Dale Anderson was born in Newton Aycliffe, County Durham, and began his career in the youth system of nearby Darlington. He made his senior debut on 4 May 1987, away to Chesterfield in the Third Division, at the age of 16 years and 254 days, which made him the club's youngest ever first-team player, a record he held for 21 years until it was broken by the 15-year-old Curtis Main against Peterborough United in May 2008.

Dale made 15 appearances in the league and three in the 1989/90 Conference championship season as manager Brian Little tended to field more experienced players.

In June 1990, the forward joined Middlesbrough, in the Second Division. He was signed with the intention of beginning his career in their reserves. Unfortunately, he never broke through to the first team and went on to play non-league football for clubs including King's Lynn, Shildon and West Auckland Town.

I met Dale at an event in 1987. We got chatting and we became firm friends and remain so to this day.

His character featured in the film based on my life, *Give Them Wings*.

My Memorable Match Involving Dale Anderson
Chesterfield v Darlington – 1985/86

By the time Darlington visited Chesterfield, they had already been relegated to the Fourth Division. Ian made the journey with another couple in their car.

Once there, the pair of us left the couple to their own devices and went for a few pints in the Chesterfield supporters' club, before heading into the ground.

From the disabled area, the two of us witnessed a typical end-of-season match.

Tony Coyle drilled a right-footed shot for the home side from the edge of the area low into the bottom corner in the second minute. It was the only goal of the game.

The only noteworthy event from my point of view was that Dale Anderson, a 16-year-old trainee, became at the time the youngest player to represent Darlington that day.

* * *

David Currie – Career Details

David Currie played as a striker for Middlesbrough, Darlington, Barnsley, Nottingham Forest, Oldham Athletic, Rotherham United, Huddersfield Town, Carlisle United and Scarborough.

David joined Barnsley from Darlington, where he'd scored 33 goals in 76 games in 1988, and played 80 league games for them, scoring 30 goals.

He signed for Nottingham Forest in January 1990 and made his debut for them on 3 February, although in August 1990 he moved again to join Oldham Athletic after falling out with Brian Clough.

My Memorable Match Involving David Currie

Darlington v Exeter City – 1987/88

I went to this match with Ian on what was an absolutely freezing afternoon. I was really pleased that I'd made the effort to go as the pair of us saw Darlington achieve their biggest victory of the season.

The Quakers were ahead as early as the third minute. Garry MacDonald made progress down the wing and played the ball inside to Mark Hine, who drove his shot across visiting keeper John Shaw and inside the far post. Eight minutes later, it was almost two as a Peter Robinson back header from an Alan Roberts corner was cleared off the line by visiting defender Ray Carter. The one-way traffic continued and Kevin Stonehouse, who is now sadly no longer with us, was the next to go close in the 17th minute when he crashed a header against the bar after a superb chip by Currie. Then it was MacDonald's turn, as he saw his header blocked on the line and shortly afterwards Shaw made a brilliant double save to keep out his follow-up effort and also one from Roberts. Darlington continued to pour forward and increased their lead on 37 minutes when Currie latched on to a Hine through pass and calmly side-footed the ball past Shaw's despairing dive. Three minutes later Currie made it 3-0 with the goal of the game. Receiving the ball wide on the left, he cut inside two defenders and unleashed a powerful drive past the helpless keeper from just outside the box.

The total domination continued after the break and on the hour Currie turned provider to set up the fourth goal. He skated past Richard Massey to the byline and crossed for Roberts to smash home from two yards out. Exeter grabbed a consolation goal on 77 minutes when Simon Mitton prodded home following a goalmouth scramble but they finished the match a well beaten side. They never came to terms with the icy surface and couldn't handle Currie, whose balance and tricky skills seemed unaffected by the frozen conditions.

As Ian pushed me back to his car, I thought about David Currie's performance. He was simply brilliant that afternoon and produced a display that still stands out in my mind to this day.

* * *

Gary Hyde – Career Details

Gary Hyde made 47 appearances in the Football League as a forward for Darlington and Scunthorpe United. He was also on the books of Leicester City during the 1990/91 season and later went on to play non-league football for Whitby Town.

While at Darlington, Gary was a member of the squad that won the 1989/90 Conference title.

My Memorable Match Involving Gary Hyde

Darlington v Oldham Athletic, League Cup first round first leg – 1988/89

I went to this match with Ian; we were lucky enough to see a really good performance from Darlington.

The hosts made a bright start and piled the pressure on their lofty opponents. Visiting keeper Andy Rhodes had a busy opening few minutes as he kept out early attempts by Paul Clayton, Garry MacDonald and Kevin Stonehouse. However, he was left helpless after seven minutes as the home side grabbed the lead. MacDonald made progress down the right. He held off Oldham centre-half Earl Barrett and squared the ball to an unmarked Gary Hyde in the box. The youngster made no mistake from 12 yards out to score his first goal for the club. Unfortunately, ten minutes later, Darlington's captain Dave Moore was forced off with a pulled hamstring. Dale Anderson came off the bench to play up front with MacDonald switching to the back four. The home side increased their lead on 27 minutes when Hyde chipped the ball forward to Clayton, who cleverly dummied Ian Marshall before drilling a powerful drive past Rhodes into the net.

The Second Division team stepped up the pace in the second half and looked much more threatening but the Darlington back line held firm with Neil Robinson superb at right-back and Jim Willis and MacDonald proving to be unbeatable in the centre of defence. Darlington always carried a threat going forward with Clayton's pace and aggression troubling the visitors. There was no further scoring as the Quakers took a two-goal lead into the second leg, which unfortunately they lost 4-0.

As I sat in the pub with my friend, I couldn't help but think that young Gary Hyde played really well and was the difference between the two teams on the night. One goal and an assist certainly backed that up. Whenever I think or talk about him, this match springs to mind.

* * *

Gary Worthington – Career Details

Gary Worthington, who is the nephew of former England international Frank, was a youth player with Manchester United. He didn't make any first-team appearances for them and eventually moved on to Huddersfield Town. He also played in the Football League for Darlington, Wrexham, Wigan Athletic, Exeter City and Doncaster Rovers.

He later played non-league football with Halifax Town.

After retiring from playing, Gary worked in youth development for Leeds United and Chelsea. He later joined Manchester City as their head of player recruitment.

My Memorable Match Involving Gary Worthington
Colchester United v Darlington – 1988/89

On 25 November 1988 I went with Ian to Layer Road, Colchester. We travelled on the supporters' coach, setting off at about nine in the morning. When we arrived at the ground, we went straight to their supporters' club bar, which was up a flight of stairs. Ian and some other lads lifted me up in my wheelchair.

From a window you could see out over the pitch. I said to Ian, 'This game is never going to go ahead.' Thick fog rolling in from the North Sea made visibility very difficult for the sparse crowd of only 1,550. The referee gave the go-ahead only half an hour before the match was due to start.

Inside the ground we met up with Stephen Lowson and saw John Gray and Richard Jones who were also there. A steward then told us that the referee was insisting that it was no good having fans behind any of the goals due to the poor visibility. Instead, everyone was moved to the main stand, with Ian carrying me up to one of the wooden bench seats.

Even so, from my vantage point I couldn't see either set of goalposts. Nevertheless, despite the atrocious conditions, Gary Worthington scored a penalty for the Quakers after 25 minutes, then added a second after 63 with Radford scoring Colchester's consolation goal in the 72nd minute.

After the game, we had a few celebratory drinks in Colchester before we caught a train back to London where we were staying at Stephen's house.

On the train to Stephen's, although I hadn't seen the game very clearly, I'd seen enough of Gary Worthington during the game to come to the conclusion that he was Darlington's best player on the night, by some distance. Not only did he score two goals, but his overall forward play had been excellent.

Apart from the fog, this fact stuck in my mind and has done to this day.

* * *

David Cork – Career Details

David Cork was born in Doncaster. He played representative football at district and county schools level, and had a trial with his hometown club Doncaster Rovers, before signing schoolboy forms with Arsenal in 1978. He turned professional in 1980 and the same year spent time on loan at Swedish second-tier club GAIS. Mainly a reserve team player during his time at Arsenal, Cork helped them win the Football Combination title in 1983/84. He made his first team debut on 17 December 1983 against Watford in the First Division, a game that Arsenal won 3-1. He made eight appearances during that season, the last of which was against Liverpool on 11 February 1984, and scored once, against Southampton in December 1983. Unfortunately, he did not play a single first-team match during the 1984/85 season and was released in the summer of 1985.

Cork signed for Second Division club Huddersfield Town, under the management of Mick Buxton. He made his debut in the opening match of the season and scored their 4,000th league goal a week later, finishing the season with eight goals from 38 league appearances. Two of his nine goals in 1986/87 came in a 3-0 win at home to Millwall in the final fixture, which Huddersfield had needed to win to be sure of avoiding relegation. Against a background of changes at managerial and board level, the team spent much of 1987/88 in the relegation places. David played in the club-record 10-1 loss to Manchester City and was transfer-listed at his own request in March 1988.

He spent a month on loan to West Bromwich Albion of the Second Division across September and October 1988. He also had a trial with First Division Norwich City later in the year, before joining his former manager Mick Buxton at Scunthorpe United in February 1989 on a non-contract basis. He made 15 Fourth Division appearances as the Iron fell just short of automatic promotion, and played in both legs of the play-off semi-final defeat to Wrexham.

David then moved into non-league football with Darlington. He missed only one match as Darlington won the 1989/90 Conference title and with it promotion to the Fourth Division and scored 12 league goals. David helped his club gain a second successive promotion, scoring in the last match of the 1990/91 season, a 2-0 win against Rochdale that confirmed the Quakers as champions but in 1991/92 his contribution was not enough to prevent their relegation back to the Fourth Division. He spent the beginning of the following season with Boston in the Conference and later played for Worksop Town.

In 2013, David was living in his hometown of Doncaster, where he worked as a machinist for an aluminium manufacturer.

My Memorable Match Involving David Cork
Darlington v Boston United – 1989/90

I went to this match with Ian on what was a horrible, windy night. We saw David Cork miss a glorious chance after only 16 seconds. Kevan Smith found him with a superb long pass but with just the keeper to beat Cork side-footed wide of the post. John Borthwick was next to try his luck on ten minutes. A flowing six-man move finished with Jim Willis crossing to the far post towards the centre-forward, who headed just wide. Play became ragged and disjointed as both sides struggled with the heavy pitch and the appalling weather. Just when it looked as if Boston might hold out until half-time, a mistake by their player-manager on 39 minutes presented the Quakers with their opening goal. Dave Cusack tried to play a square ball across his defence which was read by Borthwick. He intercepted the ball and played in Cork who drove his shot into the bottom corner of the net from the edge of the box.

It took the home side just 90 seconds of the second half to increase their lead. Les McJannet crossed from the right towards Borthwick who challenged two defenders in the air. The ball fell kindly for Paul Emson who smashed it past John McKenna in the visitors' goal. Darlington were in complete control by now and went looking for more goals. McJannet played a clever one-two with Cork and thundered a shot against the post and then on 55 minutes they grabbed their third goal. A Frank Gray free kick was flicked on by David Corner and Cork lifted the ball into the roof of the net.

Two minutes later it was 4-0 as Andy Toman found Borthwick unmarked in the box and he slammed the ball past the helpless McKenna. Three minutes later Cork completed his hat-trick with the goal of the night. He prevented the ball from running out for a goal kick and from a position on the byline he wriggled past three defenders before firing his shot high into the net from the narrowest of angles. Cork claimed his fourth of the night and completed an eight-minute second half hat-trick when he scored again on 62 minutes. McJannet played a pinpoint pass from the right wing, which was collected by Cork, who held off a defender and fired into the bottom corner from ten yards out. Boston managed a consolation goal in the 85th minute when a mistake by substitute Drew Coverdale let in visiting centre-forward John McGinley who fired home with Boston's first and only effort on target.

As Ian pushed me to his car, I couldn't believe how good David Cork had been. His performance was simply awesome in a night that I'll never forget.

* * *

John Borthwick – Career Details

John Borthwick made 225 appearances in the Football League as a forward for Hartlepool United, Darlington and York City.

John joined Hartlepool in 1982 and made his debut on 3 January 1983 in a 4-1 defeat away at Colchester United. He spent six seasons with Pools, scoring 16 goals from 135 games in all competitions.

He then moved on to Darlington, newly relegated to the Conference for the 1989/90 season. His 19 goals made him the Quakers' leading scorer as they won the championship and returned to the Football League. John was again their top scorer as they won back-to-back titles to gain promotion to the Third Division. He stayed for one more season with Darlington and then spent the 1992/93 season with York City. He returned to non-league football with Gateshead. John fittingly ended his 15-year career by winning the FA Vase with Whitby Town in 1997.

My Memorable Match Involving John Borthwick
Darlington v Halifax Town, FA Cup second round – 1989/90

As per the norm, I sat in the East Stand Paddock with Ian to watch this match.

We witnessed a one-sided affair with the Quakers in complete control throughout, home goalkeeper Mark Prudhoe not having a single shot to save throughout the whole game. The Halifax goal was under constant threat from as early as the third minute when John Borthwick crashed a volley just wide of the post. Drew Coverdale was next to try his luck but fired just over the bar when well placed. Shortly after, Paul Emson had a far post header deflected wide for a corner. Darlington took the lead on 31 minutes after a defensive mix-up from the visitors. Keeper Paul Whitehead rolled the ball out to John Bramhall but then picked up his back-pass under pressure from Borthwick, resulting in an indirect free kick just inside the area. Andy Toman rolled the ball square to Coverdale, who drilled a low shot through the wall and into the net. The home side's dominance continued with David Cork and Borthwick both missing good chances before Coverdale had an effort cleared off the line.

Another defensive mix-up by the visitors handed the Quakers a second goal on 51 minutes. Whitehead and full-back Brian Butler got in each other's way dealing with a cross and the loose ball ran kindly for Les McJannet who coolly back-heeled it into an empty net from six yards out. Borthwick almost made it 3-0 but Whitehead made amends for his earlier mistakes with a stunning save. The third goal did however arrive on 67 minutes after a great run down the left by Coverdale. He beat three defenders to reach the byline and pulled the ball back to Borthwick who picked his spot from eight yards out and simply passed the ball home. From then on, Darlington went into cruise control and easily saw the game out against what was a very poor visiting team.

As I sat in the pub reading my programme, I thought that John Borthwick had been excellent throughout the match and could have had three or four goals. He was a constant threat to the Halifax defence and in my opinion, had been the best player on the pitch that day.

* * *

Lee Ellison – Career Details

Lee Ellison played in the Football League for Darlington, Hartlepool United (on loan), Leicester City, Crewe Alexandra and Hereford United.

Lee started his career at Darlington and was a regular goalscorer in their youth team before stepping up to the first team where he banged in 17 goals in 72 matches.

In 1994, he followed former Darlington manager Brian Little to Leicester City but failed to make an appearance while he was there.

At the time of writing, Lee is a successful businessman in the north-east.

My Memorable Match Involving Lee Ellison

Darlington v Fulham – 1991/92

I went to this match with the ever loyal Ian, where we witnessed a very good Darlington display.

The Quakers started brightly and dominated the early stages and took the lead in the 20th minute. Andy Toman's corner was dropped by Fulham keeper Jim Stannard and in the ensuing scramble Kevan Smith fired a shot towards goal. Dugald McCarrison got his head on to the ball and diverted it on to the post, the rebound falling invitingly for Lee Ellison who netted from ten yards out. The visitors' goal led a charmed life as Darlington remained on top and went looking for more goals. Mitch Cook saw his 20-yard free kick tipped over the bar by Stannard and then Toman rattled the post from 25 yards out. Ellison raced clear but his low shot towards the bottom corner was superbly saved by Stannard at full stretch, then Toman had a fierce shot deflected wide for a corner and McCarrison fired just over the bar with an acrobatic overhead kick from close range. Fulham hit back in the closing minutes of the first half and Mark Prudhoe was called into action for the first time. He made a good save to keep out a low drive from Peter Scott, and moments later he had to be alert to block a close range Gary Brazil header.

The visitors started the second half in a determined mood and equalised on 49 minutes with their best move of the game. A quick break down the right ended with a deep cross beyond the far post by full-back John Marshall. It was headed back across goal by Glen Thomas and headed home by Brazil for his tenth goal of the season. Just when it looked as if Fulham might take something from the game, the Quakers regained the lead on the hour mark with a brilliant piece of play by Ellison. There seemed very little on for the centre-forward when he received the ball on the edge of the box with a crowded goalmouth in front of him, but he floated the deftest of chips over the defenders into the far top corner of the net with Stannard helpless. Three minutes later Darlington made the game safe with a superbly worked team goal. Smith and Toman combined to send Cook racing away down the left and his low cross was turned into the net at the far post by McCarrison. A brilliant afternoon for the home team was tarnished slightly by the dismissal of McCarrison on 78 minutes. He felt that he'd been stamped on after a robust tackle by Scott and kicked out in retaliation. The referee missed the original incident and only saw the retaliation so waved the red card.

While Ian drove me home, I couldn't get over how good Lee Ellison had been. His second strike would have won the goal of the season award if it had been on *Match of the Day* and still is in my memory to this day.

* * *

Robbie Painter – Career Details

Robbie Painter was only 16 when he made his Football League debut as a substitute for Chester City at Bristol City on 21 November 1987. Although he appeared again from the bench a fortnight later against Doncaster Rovers, Painter then had to wait more than a year for his next first-team action. He began to play regularly towards the end of the 1988/89 season and remained involved in first team duties for the next two years but at the end of the 1990/91 season he opted to join Fourth Division club Maidstone United for an initial £30,000 along with team-mate Neil Ellis.

After less than a year at Maidstone, Robbie returned north by joining Burnley for £25,000, helping them clinch the Fourth Division title. He holds the honour of scoring the division's last goal before the leagues were rebranded in the summer of 1992. A year later he moved on again to Darlington in another £25,000 deal. His three year-stint at Feethams included an appearance at Wembley in the 1996 Third Division play-off final against Plymouth Argyle, where Darlington suffered a 1-0 defeat.

The striker moved in October 1996 to Rochdale, where his former Chester team-mate Graham Barrow was manager. He spent three years at Spotland and then moved across the Pennines to Halifax Town, where he played his final Football League match, against Darlington on 28 April 2001.

He later played for non-league sides Gateshead, Bradford Park Avenue, Ossett Town, Emley and Guiseley.

At the time of writing, Robbie is a chartered physiotherapist in Leeds, and has started dealing in property recently.

My Memorable Match Involving Robbie Painter

Darlington v Bury – 1995/96

I went to this match with Ian. The two of us had the pleasure to see what can only be described as a 'vintage performance' from our team.

We were celebrating as early as the 13th minute, as the Quakers took a deserved lead. Bury failed to clear a Steve Gaughan corner properly and it was hooked towards the far post by Andy Crosby, where it was met by Matt Carmichael who volleyed into the net past visiting keeper Lee Bracey. In their next attack a Phil Brumwell corner was headed powerfully against the bar by Crosby, then in the 17th minute Robbie Blake doubled the home side's lead. He played a one-two with Brumwell down the right before cleverly controlling the return pass and clinically dispatching the ball across the keeper into the far corner of the net. Bury rarely threatened, although Pugh and Daws both wasted opportunities for them at the end of the first half.

Darlington started the second half in fine style and the game threatened to become a rout. In the 46th minute Gaughan fired a 20-yard shot just wide and then a minute later had a strong claim for a penalty turned down.

Blake could then have added to the lead with three chances in quick succession. Firstly, he headed straight at the keeper from a Robbie Painter cross, then two minutes later he just failed to slide home a Bannister cross. In the 59th minute he hit a superb, low 20-yard drive that was brilliantly tipped away by Bracey. Bury should have found a way back into the game on the hour mark. A long free kick by Jackson was handled in the box by Brumwell, but keeper Paul Newell comfortably saved Mark Carter's awful spot-kick. Darlington continued to outplay their opponents and Painter made it 3-0 in the 67th minute. He latched on to a long through ball from Carmichael and angled a low drive into the bottom corner of the net. Anthony Carss then blazed inches wide from just outside the box and Blake shaved the bar with a blistering effort at the end of a mazy run. The fourth goal eventually arrived and it was Painter again with his second of the afternoon. He ran on to a clever angled pass from Gaughan to beat Bracey with ease from ten yards out. There was still time for Blake to go close with a shot across goal and Gary Bannister to shave the upright with a 20-yard blockbuster.

As Ian and I left the ground, the match quickly went through my mind. I have to say that Robbie Painter had an excellent game. He literally tore the Bury defence to bits. They simply couldn't deal with him during the whole game.

* * *

Robbie Blake – Career Details

Robbie Blake is at the time of writing a coach at Bognor Regis Town. He began as a striker but was increasingly used as midfielder in the latter part of his career.

Robbie began his professional career with Darlington in 1994 and went on to make more than 500 appearances in the Football League and Premier League for Bradford City, Nottingham Forest, Burnley, Birmingham City, Leeds United, Bolton Wanderers and Doncaster Rovers.

The striker was the subject of many transfers throughout his career, with career total transfer fees reaching £3.6m.

My Memorable Match Involving Robbie Blake

Scunthorpe United v Darlington – 1995/96

I accompanied Ian to the final match of the season at Scunthorpe United. This was a game that the Quakers simply had to win to have a chance of clinching automatic promotion from the Third Division.

We left quite early at about 11 in the morning and soon found ourselves in the midst of a convoy of cars, making the same journey as ourselves. The *Northern Echo* later spoke of 2,000 Darlington fans travelling to Humberside.

When we arrived in Scunthorpe at around one o'clock, we parked the car near the Berkeley, a pub not far from the ground, and interestingly, we saw the fans from both clubs sitting outside in the bright sunshine. Not a bad word was said. Anyway, after a few pints, we made our way to Glanford Park.

Luckily, Ian managed to get me into the away end without any problems where we bumped into Stephen at half-time when the score was 2-0 to the Iron with goals from John Eyre in the fourth and 35th minutes. I have to say that Darlington, in my opinion, had been poor in the first 45 minutes.

The Quakers were much better in the second period and defender/midfielder Matty Appleby converted a penalty in the 61st minute which sparked off a mass brawl among the home fans that spilled on to the pitch. After Anthony Carss's looping header found the net in the 68th minute there was yet another pitch invasion, this time from the Darlington fans. Then Andy McFarlane scored for the Iron in the 87th minute only for Mark Barnard to equalise a minute later. The nearest we came to getting the winner that we desperately needed was when a shot from Robbie Blake, who had been excellent throughout the whole game, smacked against the bar in the dying seconds.

This result meant that Darlington had to be content with a place in the play-offs.

My lasting memory of the match was Robbie Blake hitting the bar. 'If only,' I thought as I fell asleep in Ian's front seat.

* * *

Glenn Naylor – Career Details

Glenn Naylor made more than 300 appearances in the Football League for York City and Darlington. He was forced to retire in 2003 due to injury.

At the time of writing, Glenn works on the production line at Portakabin in York. When chatting to him, he informed me that he's been with them for 18 years.

My Memorable Match Involving Glenn Naylor

Darlington v Doncaster Rovers – 1996/97

I went to this match with Ian. With the East Stand being closed for demolition; we watched the game from the West Stand instead.

The pair of us saw Darlington make a bright start and dominate the early play but struggle to turn their superiority into goals. In the very first minute Mark Barnard fired in a shot from 25 yards that Rovers keeper Dean Williams superbly tipped over the bar. Williams was at full stretch again after 11 minutes to make a similar save, this time from Darren Roberts. Midfielder Simon Davey headed home a Carl Shutt cross but saw it disallowed due to some pushing in the box, before Davey and Shutt both tested the keeper with good shots. The goal that Darlington had been threatening finally arrived in the 43rd minute when Glenn Naylor slotted home from close range after a Roberts shot had been blocked and fallen invitingly at his feet. The hard-earned lead lasted for only two minutes though as Rovers equalised with the last attack of the half. A long ball forward was flicked on by Adie Mike into the path of Prince Moncrieffe, who ran through a static home defence and tucked the ball past David Preece.

The second half was only five minutes old when Darlington regained the lead as a Davey corner was headed powerfully home by Jason de Vos from six yards out. Twenty minutes later the home side added a third with a carbon copy of their second. A Davey corner was again headed home by De Vos from almost exactly the same position. The game was over as a contest three minutes later when Rovers were reduced to ten men after a shocking high tackle in the middle of the park by Harvey Cunningham on midfielder Kenny Lowe that resulted in a 20-man brawl.

The Quakers were now in complete control and went looking for more goals. Simon Shaw rattled the bar from ten yards out, Lowe dribbled his way past three defenders and shot into the keeper's hands and Shaw had a goal disallowed for offside. The fourth goal eventually arrived on 85 minutes from another corner. De Vos and Richard Hope challenged keeper Williams to the high ball at the far post and as the ball dropped loose in the area De Vos hooked it back over his shoulder across the face of goal where Shutt headed home his first goal of the season. The home side completed the scoring in the final minute when substitute Brian Atkinson found space in the box and squared the ball to an unmarked Shaw, who calmly passed the ball into the net from six yards out.

As I sat in the pub waiting for Ian to bring me my drink, I thought about what had been an excellent result for Darlington. Glenn Naylor set the ball rolling when he scored the first goal of the game which proved to be pivotal.

* * *

Peter Duffield – Career Details

Peter Duffield began his career as an 18-year-old with Sheffield United in 1987. In his time at Bramall Lane he made 58 league appearances and scored 16 goals, including a perfect penalty record of seven scored from seven taken. His last league start was on 10 December 1989 when he broke his leg at Swindon Town. He went on loan to six clubs in as many years, namely Halifax Town, Rotherham United, Blackpool, Bournemouth, Crewe Alexandra and Stockport County.

In September 1993 he joined Scottish club Hamilton Academical, where he made his name. In two years at Douglas Park he scored 38 goals in 72 league appearances.

After leaving Hamilton in 1995, Duffield went on to play for four other Scottish clubs – Airdrie, Raith Rovers, Morton and Falkirk.

In 1999, he signed for Darlington on loan, and later that year made the transfer permanent. He was on the move again the following year, joining York City.

Peter then moved to Boston United for a season, before joining Carlisle United in 2004. After the Cumbrian club suffered relegation to the Conference, he joined Conference North side Alfreton Town, where he stayed for two years.

Duffield joined Retford United in 2006 as player-assistant manager. At the close of the 2006/07 season, he was named their manager but still continued as a player.

In September 2011, Peter replaced Tommy Taylor as manager of Belper Town, and later resigned after a 5-1 defeat at Buxton in September 2014. He went on to manage Handsworth Parramore between October 2014 and January 2016.

My Memorable Match Involving Peter Duffield
Darlington v Halifax Town – 1999/2000

I went to this match with Ian and Simon. The three of us watched a brilliant game from the disabled area in the East Stand.

Despite the atrociously muddy conditions, the Quakers played brilliantly from the kick-off. Interestingly, winger Neil Heaney enjoyed a roving midfield role, which mesmerised the Halifax defence.

After 25 minutes, full-back Paul Heckingbottom was tripped in the box by Halifax defender Michael Williams and Marco Gabbiadini blasted his spot-kick into the roof of the net. Thirteen minutes later, the same defender brought down Heaney in the area and Gabbiadini tucked away his second penalty into the bottom corner. The fans in the Tin Shed then chanted, 'The referee's a hero!'

Two minutes before half-time Heaney hit a cracking shot right into the top corner, for what was an excellent goal.

A minute after the restart, Heaney delivered a perfect right-wing cross for Peter Duffield to head into the roof of the net from only six yards out. The massacre was complete and the players left the field to a standing ovation, while former Darlington players Steve Gaughan and Robbie Painter trudged off dejectedly. It was sad in a way to see these two trooping off like that as they were loyal players in their time at Darlington. Robbie, in particular, had always been a favourite of mine and still remains so to this day.

As I sat in my living room reading my programme and looking back over the game, I was of the opinion that Peter Duffield had been the perfect foil for Marco Gabbiadini and had fully deserved his goal.

* * *

Marco Gabbiadini – Career Details
Marco Gabbiadini started his professional career at York City as an apprentice at the age of 16 in 1984 and made his debut aged

17 as a substitute against Bolton Wanderers in March 1985. His full debut came on the first day of the 1985/86 season when he scored in a home win against Plymouth Argyle. Marco's talent was spotted immediately and by the end of the season, York manager Denis Smith advised England manager Bobby Robson to call him into the England under-21 team in order to avoid him being tied to playing for Italy, the birthplace of his father He became the youngest player to score a hat-trick for York, at the age of 18 in an Associate Members' Cup victory against Darlington in November 1986. From then on he quickly established himself in the first team and went on to notch 18 goals in 50 starts and 21 substitute appearances for the Minstermen.

The departure of manager and mentor Denis Smith would see Gabbiadini leave York in order to follow Smith to Sunderland for a transfer fee of £80,000 on 23 September 1987. Sunderland had been relegated to the Third Division and needed a goalscorer to help fire them back into the Second Division and the forward was seen by Smith as the perfect signing. Despite this Gabbiadini's move was seen as risky, as in order to raise funds to sign him Smith had to sell one of Sunderland's most popular players, midfielder Mark Proctor, to Sheffield Wednesday.

Gabbiadini made his Sunderland debut in a 2-0 defeat to Chester City at Roker Park. His first goals would come only three days later in a 3-0 victory over Fulham at Craven Cottage as he scored twice, a feat he would match in the next two games. He would quickly establish himself as a key player and a crowd favourite for Sunderland by scoring on a regular basis, and is known in Wearside folklore as part of the 'G-Force' thanks to the partnership he struck up with Eric Gates. In his first season at the club Gabbiadini scored 21 goals in 35 league appearances to help fire Sunderland to the Third Division championship.

Marco's second season at Sunderland was just as successful in the Second Division and he proved that he could score at a higher level. He finished as their top scorer, netting 18 goals in

36 league appearances as well as five in eight cup matches. He also became the first Sunderland player to win the North-East Player of the Year award, which was decided by football writers.

Gabbiadini's next season would see his prowess in front of goal continue as his 22 goals in 49 league appearances helped clinch Sunderland's place back in the top flight. Highlights of that season included a hat-trick against Watford at Roker Park on 9 September 1989 and the goal that he is most fondly remembered for, the second in a 2-0 win over Newcastle United at St James' Park on 16 May 1990 in the play-off semi-final, clinching Sunderland's place in the Wembley final. Although Swindon Town won the game 1-0 through a Gary Bennett own goal, Sunderland went on to claim their place in the First Division as the Robins were refused entry due to a series of financial irregularities.

The striker found it more difficult in the First Division, with Gates having left and the partnership created with new signing Peter Davenport struggled to live up to the glory days of the G-Force and he found it hard to score as regularly as previous seasons. He scored nine goals in 31 games, which at the time was his lowest total for any club season, and Sunderland were relegated on the last day.

He started 1991/92 still a Sunderland player and scored five goals in nine Second Division appearances, including a spectacular six-minute hat-trick against Charlton Athletic at Upton Park on 17 September 1991. Those goals would prove to be his last for the club. His final appearance in a red and white shirt would come four days later in a 2-1 defeat to Grimsby Town at Roker Park on 21 September 1991 in. Six days later, he broke Wearside hearts by leaving the club.

Marco was sold to Crystal Palace for a club record transfer fee of £1.8m. He was seen as a replacement for Ian Wright, who had joined Arsenal for £2.5m in September.

However, Gabbiadini made just 25 starts and scored seven goals before being sold to Derby County for £1m four months later, which made the Rams the third club that he had played for in the space of a season. In a bid to mount a serious promotion challenge, Derby invested heavily in players around the period of Gabbiadini's arrival. Marco's first full season at the Baseball Ground saw him featuring up front alongside fellow million-pound strikers Paul Kitson and Tommy Johnson, signings from Leicester City and Notts County respectively. During that campaign, he was named their player of the year. He would become an established first-team player for the Rams up until the team got promoted to the Premier League.

In order to survive relegation, Derby sought to bring in new players and Gabbiadini found his first-team opportunities limited and he was also hampered by knee injuries. He played just 14 games for the Rams and saw himself being loaned out to Birmingham City and Oxford United. His loan spell at Birmingham was cut short after he suffered another injury.

Marco then decided to move abroad and signed for Greek side Panionios on a one-year contract. Unfortunately, he became unsettled and moved back to England.

On his return, he was offered a contract at Stoke City on a monthly basis. He scored once in nine appearances and he was not offered a permanent contract.

Marco returned to York on a short-term deal in order to try and resurrect his career. However he was hampered by injury and only made seven appearances, scoring one goal. He left when his contract expired in June 1998. York manager Alan Little said he could not justify a new contract for the striker.

Gabbiadini then joined his eighth club, Darlington, where he spent a further two years. He was an immediate success and went on to score more than 50 goals for the Quakers. During his second season he helped Darlington reach the play-offs, and he was also named as Sky Sports' Third Division Player of the Season. He would later be named as Darlington's greatest ever player in a poll among supporters. Marco left in June 2000 after Darlington were beaten in the Third Division play-off final and signed for Northampton Town.

During his first season with the Cobblers, Gabbiadini established himself in the first team, playing in all of their league matches and scoring a memorable goal against Cardiff City at Ninian Park where he managed to find the back of the net from the halfway line. However, he only managed to score six league goals. During the next two seasons, injuries stalled Marco's progress and he would find it more difficult to establish himself as a regular first-team player. He also found himself often used as a midfielder rather than as a striker. At the end of his third season his contract was not renewed despite him scoring 14 goals and finishing as Northampton's top scorer.

Gabbiadini's availability alerted Darlington, who offered him a contract and even let him train with them. However, he decided to sign for arch rivals Hartlepool United instead, scoring seven goals in 12 starts and six substitute appearances. His final two goals were in Hartlepool's 4-0 FA Cup victory over Whitby Town in November 2003. He then suffered knee injuries and was advised by doctors not to continue playing. He announced his retirement in January 2004 after making over 750 appearances in all competitions.

After retiring, Marco and his wife ran an award-winning restored Victorian hotel in York. He also runs a sports management company called Quantum Sport which represents professional footballers, international cricketers and rugby players.

My Memorable Match Involving Marco Gabbiadini
Northampton Town v Darlington – 1999/2000

I went with Ian in his car. I was pleased that we bothered to make the effort because we were lucky enough to see a very good Darlington performance.

Once inside the ground, the pair of us saw the home side start brightly and take control of the early stages. As early as the second minute Carlo Corazzin headed a corner just over the bar, then Steve Howard, the former Hartlepool striker, headed weakly into Darlington goalkeeper Mark Samways's hands when well placed. In a rare attack the Quakers had a penalty appeal turned down when Marco Gabbiadini appeared to be barged to the ground while controlling a Michael Oliver cross. Corazzin continued to look dangerous for the home side and he had another headed chance which he put straight at Samways. Then he turned provider when he beat two defenders down the right and squared the ball to Sean Parrish who fired his shot straight at Samways from 12 yards out.

Completely against the run of play, Darlington took the lead in the 17th minute. Gabbiadini picked up a loose ball 30 yards out, advanced to the edge of the penalty area and drilled a low left-footed shot into the bottom corner of the net across home keeper Keith Welch. Northampton continued to push forward but were unable to score as the visitors' goal led a charmed life. The Quakers almost increased their lead on 35 minutes when Neil Heaney won the ball on the right wing, cut inside and hit a left-footed shot straight at Welch. Darlington did score a second two minutes later with a superbly worked goal. Heaney found Gabbiadini, who'd made a run down the right. He reached the byline and cut the ball back to Jesper Hjorth, who drilled a first-time half volley into the bottom corner of the net from 12 yards out.

Darlington began the second half on the attack and trying to add to their two-goal advantage. Gabbiadini played in Hjorth who raced clear of the defence and tried to chip the keeper, but Welch read it and saved easily. A minute later Hjorth returned the favour when he set up Gabbiadini but he lost control at the vital moment with just Welch to beat. Northampton hit back with a quick free kick and a David Savage cross into the box, but Neil Aspin read the danger and made an excellent interception. The Quakers scored their third goal on 53 minutes. Gabbiadini picked up the ball in midfield and ran at the home side's penalty area. He played a neat one-two with Hjorth on the edge of the box, before twisting and turning past the last defender Hendon and passing the ball into the bottom corner of the net past the helpless Welch, in front of an impressive contingent of travelling fans. The visitors were by now in complete control and dominated the rest of the game, meaning the home side never really threatened to get back into it.

I have to say, Marco Gabbiadini was the difference between the two sides. As I fell asleep in Ian's front seat, I thought that Darlington were extremely lucky to have in their team. Anyone who saw David Hodgson's side that season certainly wouldn't argue that point.

* * *

Danny Mellanby – Career Details

Danny Mellanby played for Bishop Auckland, Crook Town, West Auckland, Darlington (twice) and Newton Aycliffe.

He played 44 league games, scoring nine times for the Quakers between 2001 and 2004.

Danny also featured for Bishop Auckland in 2000 and 2001. In addition, he was a member of Alan Oliver's Crook Town side that reached the FA Vase quarter-finals in 2006.

The striker also served under Oliver at West Auckland and later hit 15 goals in 50 Northern League appearances for Newton Aycliffe.

In June 2012 Danny rejoined Darlington. Three months later he returned to Newton Aycliffe.

On 12 January 2015, he was appointed manager of Northern League Division Two club Northallerton Town after being appointed assistant in November 2014.

My Memorable Match Involving Danny Mellanby

Darlington v Exeter City –2001/02

I went with Ian and we watched the proceedings from our usual position in the new East Stand.

We saw Darlington make a bright opening which resulted in them taking the lead after only five minutes. Danny Mellanby left two City defenders for dead with a clever turn in the box and a pass across the face of goal that was tapped home by winger Richard Hodgson. Shortly after, Mellanby went close to increasing the lead twice; he fired one chance just wide then headed another effort over the bar when well placed. Exeter's only attempt of any real note was a snapshot from the edge of the box by Sean McCarthy which was well saved by Andy Collett.

The Quakers' second goal arrived on 62 minutes. A Hodgson corner was headed powerfully towards goal by winger Mark Convery. It was met on the line by Mellanby who swivelled and hooked the ball home. By this time, Darlington were in complete control and made it 3-0 five minutes later. A long clearance out of defence was latched on to by Mellanby who held off City defender Dylan Kerr and lobbed the ball over the advancing keeper from the edge of the area. It was 4-0 on 82 minutes when midfielder Mark Ford chased a ball into the box and put pressure on City keeper Arjan van Heusden who hammered his clearance against Kerr and the ball dropped perfectly for Ford to roll into the empty net. Exeter were denied a late consolation goal when Collett pulled off a superb save from a point-blank Cherif Diallo header to preserve his clean sheet.

I have to say that in my opinion, Danny Mellanby had his best game for the club and was certainly the difference between the two sides that day.

* * *

Mark Sheeran – Career Details
Mark Sheeran played 32 league games and scored six goals for Darlington between 2001 and 2004.

My Memorable Match Involving Mark Sheeran
Scunthorpe United v Darlington, Football League Trophy first round – 2001/02

I went on the train with Ian. The two of us left Darlington at midday, arriving in Doncaster at one o'clock. We therefore decided to go to the Railway pub for a few drinks before continuing our journey to Scunthorpe.

After a few hours we were on our travels again, this time catching a local train for the remainder of our journey.

Once at our destination, we hailed a cab to take us to the Berkeley, a pub near Glanford Park. After having something to eat, we headed for the ground on what was an absolutely freezing night.

To be honest, I thought on more than one occasion during the game that I'd rather be sitting at home in the warmth of my living room, listening on the radio, especially after witnessing what can only be described as a poor excuse for a match.

Manager Tommy Taylor sprang a couple of surprises in what was his first team selection for Darlo. Frank van der Geest made a rare appearance in goal and youth team striker Mark Sheeran was named among the substitutes. Unfortunately, inspirational captain Craig Liddle was out with a long-term injury. He was replaced by David Brightwell; no disrespect to him, but it wasn't exactly a like-for-like swap.

The Quakers actually started quite brightly, with Barry Conlon going the closest to scoring. Unfortunately, his strike partner Kirk Jackson looked way out of his depth hence 'Bazza' was basically having to forage up front on his own, something he'd get used to during his Darlo career.

It came as no surprise when, following a period of sustained pressure early in the second half, the hosts took the lead through Lee Hodges. Former Darlo forward Martin Carruthers quickly added a second following good work by Peter Beagrie. After that, Darlo capitulated and it became a matter of how many the Iron would score. However, their fans had to be content with only one more goal scored by Jamie McCombe, again after good work by the man of the match, the former Middlesbrough winger Peter Beagrie. As I sat on Scunthorpe station waiting for our train to Doncaster, I thought that the only good thing to come out of that match was the appearance of young Mark Sheeran. He certainly looked useful when he came on. A few days later, my intuition was correct when he came off the bench to score twice against Luton Town.

* * *

Tommy Wright – Career Details

A former England under-19 and under-20 international, Tommy Wright started his career with Leicester City, helping them into the Premier League in 2002/03. However he failed to hold down a regular first-team place at the higher level and was loaned out to Brentford and Blackpool. He signed for Barnsley in 2006 and helped the club gain promotion out of League One via the play-offs. The striker joined Darlington in January 2007 following a short loan spell at League Two champions Walsall. After a year, he was sold on to Scottish Premier League side Aberdeen in August 2008 for £100,000. He returned to England in January 2010, signing with Grimsby Town, who were soon relegated out of the Football League. He rejoined Darlington, helping the club to lift the 2011 FA Trophy. After leaving the Quakers, Tommy appeared for a string of non-league clubs, latterly as player-manager with Corby Town and Nuneaton Town. In October 2017, he joined Darlington for a third spell, this time as manager. He left them at the end of the 2018/19 season after a mid-table finish in National League North.

Tommy is now a police officer at the time of writing, having decided on a career change in December 2020.

My Memorable Match Involving Tommy Wright

Accrington Stanley v Darlington – 2007/08

I made the trip to this match on the train with Ian. We caught the 9.30 to York, where we would have to change trains, and were afforded some onboard entertainment thanks to some Americans who were already onboard. There must have been around ten of them all trying to secure seats. In addition they had around 15 pieces of luggage which couldn't be stored in the carriage. They only succeeded in blocking the entrance with what could only be described as a wall of baggage. People simply couldn't get past and tempers got rather frayed. While all this was going on Ian made a brilliant comment saying that they reminded him of 'an American version of the Dingles'.

I thought this was very apt. Anyway, on arrival at York they had to dismantle their 'wall' to let us out. The last time we saw them, they were piling up their cases and bags in the place that is supposed to be reserved for wheelchair users that we had just vacated! So much for leaving that particular space clear!

The pair of us only had eight minutes to catch our connecting train to Accrington. The same guy who had got us off the York train put us on the Accrington one with the use of a ramp.

On entering the carriage where the disabled place was situated, we noticed that there was an old couple sitting in the wheelchair space. They kindly offered to move, but that was only the half of it! After they had done so, Ian noticed that the seat where the lady had been sitting stank of urine and was damp! So obviously he sat on the one next to it. Unfortunately for him, at Bradford another wheelchair user got on the train. Since she could walk a little Ian had to move along to let her sit down, meaning he had to use the smelly seat. Luckily for him, we had a newspaper with us and he put it over the seat before sitting on it. I still found the whole situation highly amusing, especially when I saw the expression on my friend's face when he had to switch seats! It was priceless!

Anyway, we arrived in Accrington without further incident and on leaving the train we headed to the Railway for a pint. They had the football on, Portsmouth versus Bolton Wanderers. The Trotters looked poor despite taking the lead. Portsmouth eventually won 3-1. The pub was alright but after the footie we decided to move on, this time to the Nags Head where the two of us had something to eat (steak and chips for me). After a couple more pints we headed to the ground in a taxi with another couple of Darlington fans who had also been in the pub.

On arrival at the ground we said goodbye to our fellow passengers before going to pick up the complimentary tickets from reception that Neil Wainwright had kindly left us. After we had collected them we went to the supporters' bar for a swift half before taking our places in the disabled area to watch the game.

The Quakers started really brightly with winger Chris Palmer causing all sorts of problems down the left. However, it was the home side who had the first couple of chances, both of which were easily dealt with by the ever improving David Stockdale. Firstly, he grabbed a swirling John Miles cross in mid-air and then shortly afterwards he kept hold of a free kick from the same player. After these two efforts it was the visitors who took the game by the scruff of the neck and it came as no surprise when they took the lead after 26 minutes. Rob Purdie crossed from the right, and Tommy Wright outjumped everyone to plant a header firmly into the back of the net. Purdie, for me deserved a lot of praise for the sheer quality of the cross. It made Wright's task easy.

Darlington continued to press and Ricky Ravenhill had a shot blocked after good work by Wright to set up the chance. Unfortunately, Ravenhill took a knock shortly after that and was replaced by Michael Cummins who slotted into the midfield with no problems. Despite creating several other chances, one goal was all Darlington had to show for what was a very good first-half display.

At half-time Ian and I returned to the bar. By the time he got served, it was almost time for the second half to kick off. Unbelievably, I missed a Darlington goal! Ian saw it through the window of the bar. Apparently, Palmer was the provider; he crossed from the left where Abbott was on hand to slot the ball home from close range. It goes without saying that my friend found it highly amusing that I'd missed the goal. I was slightly disappointed but it wasn't the end of the world and at least I hadn't sat on a damp, urine-smelling seat earlier in the day – that was far funnier to me. Anyway, once I mentioned that fact he seemed to shut up rather rapidly.

By the time we got back to our place almost 60 minutes had gone. I wasn't particularly bothered as while I was finishing my drink Ian was commentating from his vantage point, this being his window seat. Anyway, Darlington by this stage were completely in control and Abbott was causing the Accrington defence all sorts of trouble with his pace – they simply couldn't handle him. Twice he left them for dead before shooting wide. Ian and I were just about to leave when substitute Gregg Blundell, who had come on for Tommy Wright, made a surging run into the box and was pulled down by an Accrington defender. The referee immediately pointed to the spot and Abbott grabbed the ball before smashing it into the net to round off an excellent victory.

It had been a really good result for Darlington. Tommy Wright had been excellent prior to being substituted and had been an excellent foil for Pawel Abbott. In addition, he'd set the Quakers on their way to victory by scoring their first goal.

* * *

Shaun Reay – Career Details

Shaun Reay started his career with Darlington on a youth contract and impressed so much so that he was given his first professional deal on 13 October 2006, an 18-month agreement which would expire at the end of the 2007/08 season.

Although Shaun played at junior and reserve level, he made only four appearances for Darlington's first team. In the 2006/07 season he started one game and came on as a substitute twice, and the following season he made only one substitute appearance. On 22 May 2008, Reay was released from his contract by manager Dave Penney. A few weeks later, Penney announced that the club had in fact retained the young striker and handed him another chance, with the intention of sending him out on loan to gain experience.

Reay signed for Conference North club Harrogate Town on loan for the 2008/09 season. While with the CNG Stadium club he made eight appearances, starting one game and coming on as a substitute in the other seven.

Blyth Spartans signed Reay on 22 October 2008 on a two-year contract after he had become frustrated at the lack of first-team opportunities at Darlington and was released. On 25 October, in a fourth qualifying round tie in the FA Cup against Sheffield FC, Shaun came off the substitutes' bench at half-time to make his debut with Blyth 1-0 down. He made a big impact, setting up the equaliser and then putting Blyth 2-1 up with an instinctive angled drive. Blyth went on to win 3-1, and Reay's cameo earned him the man of the match award. He was also nominated as the FA's player of the round for his performance. In the first round proper, Shaun scored twice as Blyth upset League Two side Shrewsbury Town 3-1, the first coming after just 31 seconds. This performance again earned him a nomination for the FA's player of the round award.

In 2008/09, his first season with Spartans, Shaun made 36 appearances, starting 27, and netted 12 goals. He was rewarded for his efforts with the club's young player of the season award.

Shildon signed Reay on 4 September 2009, with Blyth retaining his Conference North registration for the season. He made his debut on 5 September at home to Consett. Shildon lost 2-1, but after the match manager Gary Forest promised supporters that the forward would score goals. Unfortunately, he wasn't there long enough to do that.

In October 2009, Shaun joined Northern Premier League Premier Division side Whitby Town. He made his debut on 31 October 2009 against King's Lynn in a 2-0 defeat in the second qualifying round of the FA Trophy. After struggling to fit into the side, Shaun's time at the Turnbull Ground turned out to be a short one and he was released by mutual consent.

After leaving Whitby, Shaun began training with Jarrow Roofing, and signed for the club on Christmas Eve 2009. His debut was on 23 January 2010 in the Northern League Division Two match at home to Birtley Town, which Jarrow won 2-1, Reay making an assist for the winning goal. His first goals for the club came in a 5-0 win away to Crook Town on 13 February, where he grabbed a hat-trick. Jarrow were promoted to Northern League Division One at the end of the season, finishing in third place.

On 2 June 2010, Shaun joined Bedlington Terriers. He scored two goals in three pre-season outings but was used primarily as a substitute.

After Reay was made available for transfer in October 2010 he signed for Boldon Community Association where his father and uncle had recently taken over. Although Shaun missed the start of the season, he made 29 appearances (27 in the league) and netted 26 times (24 in the league), giving him a goals per game ratio of 0.9. Shaun was voted man of the match five times and, although he missed the first 11 league games, he still finished third in the league's top scorer list. In June 2012 he rejoined Darlington, and stayed there for a few months before playing for several non-league clubs, including Hebburn.

My Memorable Match Involving Shaun Reay
Darlington v Dagenham & Redbridge – 2007/08

As per the norm, I went to this match with my buddy Ian. After a couple of pints, the two of us took our places in the disabled area at the Arena.

I was pleased to see that Pawel Abbott had returned to the side following his hamstring injury, which was a good thing. He would certainly boost Darlington's attack.

Unfortunately, Abbott lasted for only 15 minutes as his hamstring appeared to have tightened and was replaced by youngster Shaun Reay. Shortly after the substitution, the Quakers took the lead. Neil Wainwright beat his man on the right before crossing for Ricky Ravenhill to head home his third goal of the season. Darlington continued to pour men forward and shortly after the goal, Reay had a good shot saved by former Queens Park Rangers and Wales keeper Tony Roberts. Just before the break, Tommy Wright shot wide after good work by Ravenhill. Dagenham never threatened the hosts' goal during the first 45 minutes and Ian and I were disappointed to be only 1-0 up at the interval.

The Quakers started the second half at a good pace and doubled their lead in the 15th minute. Reay played a one-two with Wright before lobbing the ball over Roberts for his first senior goal for the club. It did take a deflection off a Dagenham defender, but to me it was Reay's goal all the way. After that, Darlington replaced Wright with Michael Cummins and took their foot off the pedal and in the process allowed the visitors back into the game. Sam Sloma pulled a goal back after 63 minutes with what was a good finish. Two minutes later Ben Parker fouled Sam Saunders in the box and was immediately sent off by the referee who also awarded a penalty which Dave Rainford dispatched with ease to level the scores at 2-2. By this time, the hosts had lost their shape and it came as no surprise to me when Dagenham netted the winner in the 74th minute when Paul Benson's shot was deflected past David Stockdale by the luckless Clark Keltie. Stephen Foster almost equalised in the 90th minute, but Roberts brilliantly saved his header which meant that the visitors would be playing League Two football the following season.

While I was disappointed with the result and second-half performance, I was really pleased to see Shaun Reay score his first senior goal for the club. I'd always rated him and felt that he should have been given more of an opportunity at the club.

Even now, when I think of Shaun, I think of him as 'the one who got away'.

* * *

Pawel Abbott – Career Details

Pawel Abbott was born in York to a Polish mother and an English father as the younger of two children. He first played football for Beagle Boys in York before the team changed its name to York RI. He had the chance to play for Doncaster Rovers but declined the offer and moved to Poland, where he became a youth player at ŁKS Łódź, before moving back to England to join Preston North End at the age of 19.

He did not have the best time at Preston, making only 25 appearances in three years and having two loan spells at Bury.

In early 2004, Abbott was signed on loan by Huddersfield Town as a makeshift replacement for Jon Stead who had been sold to Premier League side Blackburn Rovers. He scored on his debut after coming off the bench against Bristol Rovers, going on to score four times in six games on loan. He was then bought for a fee of around £125,000. He would score only once more that season, but in 2004/05 became the first Town striker in six years to hit more than 20 goals as he struck 27 times in all competitions.

The following season was less successful for Abbott. After an initial run of scoring in six consecutive games in August and September, he suffered something of a goal drought over the remainder of the campaign, being relegated to being a bit-part player from the bench following this loss of form. He scored a total of 14 times.

In July 2006, Abbott rejected a move to Milton Keynes Dons as part of a deal – or no deal as it turned out – with their defender Dean Lewington. He said that he wanted to fight for a first-team place against Gary Taylor-Fletcher, Andy Booth, John McAliskey and new signing Luke Beckett. In his penultimate game for Huddersfield, on 30 December 2006, he scored two goals (including a last-minute winner) against the club he would ironically go on to join in a matter of days, Swansea City. In his final game, he was sent off against Doncaster Rovers on 1 January 2007.

Pawel made his debut as a late substitute against Gillingham on 23 January. He had been signed by Kenny Jackett, but shortly afterwards Jackett was replaced by Roberto Martínez. After 18 league appearances (nine starts) for the Swans, Abbott had scored just once, against Rotherham United, which was Martínez's first game in charge.

After just six months with Swansea, Abbott joined Darlington for £100,000. Here he found some of his best form scoring 17 goals from 31 appearances. However, he was prone to injuries during his two seasons at the Arena. In June 2009, Abbott signed for League One team Oldham Athletic on a two-year deal. He scored his first two goals for the club on 15 August 2009, wrapping up a 2-1 victory against Leyton Orient. Pawel finished the season as Oldham's top scorer with 13 goals.

On 30 July 2010, Abbott signed for Charlton Athletic for £20,000. He netted twice against Shrewsbury Town in the League Cup to register his first goals for the club. He went on to score against Milton Keynes Dons in the Football League Trophy and Swindon in the league, ending his season with a tally of four goals.

In February 2011, Abbott joined Polish side Ruch Chorzów on a free transfer, after playing 25 matches for Charlton and scoring four goals. He scored his first goal in July 2011 for his new club, securing a 2-1 victory over GKS Bełchatów on the first day of the 2011/12 season.

My Memorable Match Involving Pawel Abbott
Chester City v Darlington – 2007/08

By the time Darlington played their last league game of the season at Chester City, with the club being in administration, Dave Penney had decided to quit to go to Oldham Athletic and his assistant Martin Gray was put in temporary charge of team affairs.

Ian and I made the trip to the Deva Stadium, not really knowing whether it would be our last ever fixture.

As the pair of us entered the bar, some Darlington fans were close to tears and in a state of shock at what had gone on.

Personally, I wasn't as I'd seen it all before in 2003. Yes, I was disappointed with what had happened, but the club had overspent and this was the result!

Once inside the ground, Ian and I witnessed a spirited performance from the Quakers who eventually won 2-1 with both goals scored by Pawel Abbott, the winner coming with what was almost the last kick of the match.

After the game had ended, the players came out and threw their shirts into the crowd. Ian and I both knew that most of them wouldn't be at the club the following season and we were right as it happens.

Apart from the disappointment regarding the mess the club was in, my overriding memory was Pawel Abbott's performance. He was excellent throughout the whole match and deserved his two goals. It was the only bright spark in what was a hugely upsetting day for many Darlington fans, including Ian and I.

* * *

Michael Smith – Career Details

Born in Wallsend, Tyne and Wear, Michael Smith made his debut in the Football League for Darlington on 5 April 2010, replacing Chris Moore in the 77th minute of their 1-0 home defeat by Hereford United in League Two. He scored his first Football League goal on 1 May, in the 79th minute of Darlington's 2-0 away win at Macclesfield Town, a game that I attended.

He joined Conference North club Workington on loan for a month on 29 October 2010 and made seven appearances before returning to Darlington. In his first four Conference matches back with Darlington he scored six goals. At the end of the season, he signed a new two-year contract.

After trials with Watford and Stoke City, and an unsuccessful bid of £80,000 from Bristol City, Smith signed a three-year contract with League One club Charlton Athletic on 31 August 2011; the fee was undisclosed. He made his Charlton debut against FC Halifax Town in the FA Cup and came on in the 87th minute to cross for Bradley Pritchard to score the fourth goal of the match.

In January 2012, Michael joined League Two club Accrington Stanley on loan to the end of the season. Ten days later, he scored a hat-trick and provided an assist for Luke Joyce as Stanley beat Gillingham 4-3. He returned to his parent club in mid-March after suffering a season-ending knee injury.

On 14 August 2012, Smith made his first start – and what proved to be last appearance for Charlton – in a League Cup defeat to Leyton Orient. He then began a series of loan spells. In November, he joined Newport County of the Conference Premier on a one month loan and scored against Cambridge United on his debut. The loan was extended for a second month. On completion, he joined League One club Colchester United, also for a month.

In July 2013, Michael signed for League Two club AFC Wimbledon on loan until 1 January 2014. Wearing the number nine shirt, he made his debut on the opening day of the 2013/14 season in a 1-1 draw with Torquay United. He was a regular in the side, finishing his loan period with ten goals from 25 appearances.

January 2014 saw Michael sign for Swindon Town for an initial £100,000. He scored his club's first and third goals as they beat Shrewsbury Town 3-1 on his debut three days later.

On the final day of the January 2016 transfer window, Smith joined League Two club Portsmouth on a three-month loan. The move was made permanent at the end of the season for an undisclosed fee. He scored a hat-trick against Yeovil Town in an EFL Trophy tie on 30 August, though Portsmouth lost the match 4-3.

After just over a year, Smith signed a two-year contract with Bury of League One. However, in January 2018, he was on the move again when he signed for fellow League One club Rotherham United, again for an undisclosed fee.

After an impressive month in which he scored five goals, assisting two others in five matches, Smith was awarded the EFL League One Player of the Month Award for October 2021. He won the award for the second time in the season in January 2022 after scoring four of Rotherham's five goals across the month with the fifth being an own goal deflected in from his shot.

He was named as the side's player of the season for 2021/22, having scored 24 goals in all competitions at the time of the award.

On 22 June 2022, it was announced that Smith had joined Sheffield Wednesday on a free transfer following the expiration of his Rotherham contract, and he made his Wednesday debut against Portsmouth on 30 July 2022 coming off the bench for George Byers. His first goal would come against Bradford City in the EFL Trophy from the penalty spot. Following his first goal he would score back-to-back League One goals against Morecambe and Ipswich Town which would see him win Wednesday's September player of the month award. At the end of the season, Wednesday clinched promotion via the League One play-offs to the Championship.

My Memories of Michael Smith

I've known Michael since 2011. In that year he appeared as a player in our very first trailer for *Give Them Wings* in the scene where we recreated the Welling match (a game that's mentioned earlier in this book). Michael was excellent and must have headed the winning goal 50 times!

This guy is the inspiration I have to succeed in life. When he was 16, like me, Michael was struck down with meningitis. That's why it was important for me to get him involved in the aforementioned trailer.

Due to this illness, he missed over half of his time as a youth player at Darlington. However, he fought back to earn himself a professional contract and at the time of writing he is currently plying his trade for Sheffield Wednesday in the Championship. This is a fantastic testament to his hard work and determination to succeed in professional football.

One final note regarding Michael: we have remained in contact through what has been a brilliant career for him, and no one was happier than me to see him clinch promotion via the League One play-offs to the Championship at the end of the 2022/23 season.

* * *

Graeme Armstrong – Career Details

Striker Graeme Armstrong started his career in 2007 at Dunston UTS and went on to play for Gateshead, Harrogate Town,

Blyth Spartans, Whitby Town, Darlington, Spennymoor Town, South Shields and Hebburn Town, before retiring in 2021.

At the time of writing, Graeme is a PE teacher at a school in Northumberland. When chatting to him, he informed me that he has been in that position for 14 years.

My Memorable Match Involving Graeme Armstrong
Darlington v Burscough – 2014/15

I went to this match with Ian where we were lucky enough to see a very good Darlington performance.

The visitors caused the Quakers a few moments of alarm at the beginning of the first half when they had a substantial wind at their backs, but Darlington overcame this and were 2-0 up after 35 minutes and certainly good value for their lead. Goals from Amar Purewal and Graeme Armstrong had put Martin Gray's side ahead during a one-sided first half. Purewal netted his tenth league goal of the campaign on 19 minutes, completing fine build-up play to poke home from 16 yards, and he was also involved in the second goal, heading into Armstrong's path following goalkeeper Peter Jameson's long kick for his strike partner to score.

Having overcome Burscough's bright start to the second period, the Quakers sealed victory when Stephen Thompson netted a penalty with 20 minutes remaining. It came after Joe Comozzi had handled in the penalty area when winger Adam Mitchell had dribbled into the box, Thompson taking spot-kick responsibilities because defender and usual penalty taker Terry Galbraith was named among the substitutes.

As Ian and I left the ground to head home, I thought Graeme Armstrong had been the perfect partner for Amar Purewal for this match. He won lots of headers in what was an excellent performance. His goal was the icing on the cake.

* * *

Nathan Cartman – Career Details
Darlington beat several clubs to sign Nathan Cartman in January 2015, paying Harrogate Railway Athletic an undisclosed sum for him.

The striker had started his career at Leeds United and graduated through their academy.

When he was released by the Elland Road club, he played for Harrogate Town, Liversedge and Brighouse before joining Harrogate Railway Athletic. He made 130 appearances for the Rail, scoring 67 goals, and in the 2014/15 season he notched 36 goals in 35 games for them.

After leaving Darlington in 2017, Nathan joined Farsley. He later played for Scarborough.

At the time of writing, he is playing for Liversedge.

My Memorable Match Involving Nathan Cartman
Darlington v Ramsbottom United –2015/16

I went to this game with Ian and we watched from the bar at Heritage Park.

We saw Darlington make a good start and after 15 minutes, winger Anthony Bell forced the away goalkeeper into a good save at his near post. During an entertaining first half, two penalty shouts came and went for the Quakers, with the home crowd particularly incensed at a push on Graeme Armstrong. At the other end, United had a penalty appeal turned down, as well as having a goal disallowed for offside. Darlington's best chance of the first 45 minutes came late on. Stephen Thompson went past two defenders as if they weren't there and managed to get a clear shot on goal, but he was foiled by the goalkeeper.

Half-time saw the introduction of a new signing, the former Middlesbrough player Ryan Brobbel, and he played a crucial role in the opening goal. The midfielder lofted in an inswinging cross into the box for Nathan Cartman to glance into the corner of the net. Defender Alan White had come on for Armstrong just before the first goal. He played up front and grabbed a goal. A great move saw Adam Mitchell and Cartman involved, before Thompson chipped the ball to the back post for White to spectacularly volley home. Darlington, at this stage, were completely on top with Thompson twice almost adding to the total with strikes from outside the box. However, it would be a nervy final couple of minutes as Ramsbottom United pulled a goal back against the run of play. A low ball was whipped across the face of the goal and Lee Gaskell, later to play for Darlington, came in round the back to tap home. Much to my delight, Darlington held on to claim three precious points in their quest for promotion.

As Ian pushed me back to his car, we spoke about the match that we'd just seen. The pair of us agreed that Nathan Cartman had been excellent and had fully deserved his goal.

* * *

Mark Beck – Career Details

Mark Beck was born in Sunderland. He started his career in the youth team of Carlisle United and signed a two-year apprenticeship in the summer of 2010.

The striker made his professional debut for Carlisle on 14 April 2012, in a 1-0 defeat to Charlton Athletic, coming on as a substitute for Tom Taiwo. On 19 April he was offered a one-year professional contract. He scored his first goal for the club on 28 August in a 2-1 win against Ipswich Town in the League Cup with a 90th-minute header.

In March 2012, Mark joined Conference North club Workington on a one-month loan in order to gain first-team experience. He made his debut on 25 March in a 1-0 win over Harrogate Town, coming on as a substitute for Gareth Arnison and scoring the equalising goal for the Reds in a 1-1 draw with Droylsden. He made four appearances in his short spell, scoring the one goal.

On 30 January 2014, Beck joined Falkirk in the Scottish Championship on loan until the end of the season. He quickly struck up a strong partnership with Rory Loy, and after two substitute appearances he settled into a starting berth in the team. Mark scored the only goal of the match in a 1-0 away victory against Dundee on 29 March 2014 and was also the scorer of an equaliser in the Scottish Premiership play-off semi-final first leg against Hamilton Academical on 13 May 2014, converting a cut-back from Loy.

His final appearance for Falkirk came in the second-leg defeat to Hamilton, in which his team lost 1-0 to go out 2-1 on aggregate. In his five-month spell at Falkirk, Beck played 19 times in all competitions, scoring six goals.

Beck signed for Carlisle's fellow League Two club Yeovil Town on 24 July 2015 on a two-year contract. He made his debut on 8 August against Exeter City in a 3-2 defeat.

On 26 January 2016, Beck was on the move again. This time he joined National League club Wrexham on loan until the end of the season.

On his return from his loan Mark was released by Yeovil, despite having a year left on his contract.

At the start of the 2016/17 season, Beck signed for Darlington in National League North. He made his debut on 13 August, scoring in a 4-1 win over Boston United. Mark finished the season as the club's top scorer with 18 goals, all in the league. He returned to full-time football when signing for Harrogate Town, also in National League North, on 7 November 2017 for an undisclosed fee and helped them win promotion to the National League that season, before they reached the EFL in 2020.

Beck joined National League North club York City on 23 July 2021 on loan until January 2022. He scored six goals in 25 appearances in all competitions before returning to Harrogate, where he played in 17 matches, mainly as a substitute, without scoring.

He was released at the end of the season and rejoined Darlington in July 2022. His goalscoring form returned with six goals from his first eight games. His first career hat-trick helped Darlington to come back twice from behind and eliminate divisional rivals Southport from the FA Cup second qualifying round on 17 September. By January, he was the top scorer in National League North with 15 goals and had helped Darlington to third place in the table.

During the January 2023 transfer window, Solihull Moors of the National League met Beck's release clause and offered him terms beyond Darlington's reach. He therefore signed a two-and-a-half-year contract with Moors on 26 January.

At the time of writing, he's still with the same club.

My Memorable Match Involving Mark Beck
Darlington v Altrincham – 2016/17

I went to this match with Ian. I have to say, we witnessed a very good Darlington display.

The Quakers went close after only two minutes when Josh Falkingham crossed low from the left, and John Cyrus sliced a clearance over his own crossbar. The hosts scored from the corner that followed. Defender David Ferguson curled the corner into the box where David Syers helped the ball on for Mark Beck to prod home at the far post for his 13th league goal of the season.

The Quakers had another chance on nine minutes when Chris Hunter made a good run down the right and crossed into the middle where Nathan Cartman twisted well and headed just over the bar. The visitors almost equalised with their first shot at goal on 17 minutes when Elliot Newby found space and 25 yards out and aimed for the bottom corner, but Darlington goalkeeper Ed Wilczynski got down well low to his left and pushed the shot away. The home side had a goal disallowed on 23 minutes when Stephen Thompson outpaced his marker down the right and pulled the ball back for Cartman to hit towards goal, where Beck put it in the net, but the assistant's flag went up offside. Five minutes later, it was 2-0. Beck helped on a long clearance for Falkingham to race through and beat Tim Deasy with a powerful, low left-footed shot for his first Darlington goal. Altrincham pulled a goal back just after the half-hour mark when Wilczynski could only parry a left-footed shot by James Lawrie, and Newby put the loose ball into the net. 'Game on,' I thought. The Quakers hit back just on half-time and Beck headed Ferguson's corner on for Gary Brown to head against the bar. That was the last real action of what was a very entertaining first period.

The visitors' Newby had the first opportunity of the second half, a right-footed shot that went a couple of yards over the top. The game had few chances after that until the 78th minute, when Ferguson was tripped by Sam Heathcote and the referee pointed to the spot, from where defender Terry Galbraith sent the keeper the wrong way to score. This goal made history because it was the first successful Darlington penalty scored at Blackwell Meadows.

It was nearly 4-1 shortly after when Thompson crossed for Beck to head towards goal but Jones tipped the ball over. By this time, the home side were completely in control and cruised through the last ten minutes to secure the three points.

As Ian and I left the ground, I thought to myself that Mark Beck had been excellent throughout the whole game and was definitely the difference between the two teams.

* * *

Stephen Thompson – Career Details

Stephen Thompson plays as a striker for Northern Premier League Division One East club Stockton Town as of the time of writing.

Unable to make the first team at Middlesbrough, he signed for Port Vale in May 2008. He left Vale Park by mutual consent in October 2009, at which point he joined Telford United. He spent one season with them before joining Durham City. He signed for Darlington in September 2012 and helped the club to the Northern League title in 2012/13, promotion out of the Northern Premier League Division One North via the play-offs in 2015, and finally the Premier Division title in 2015/16.

Stephen was named as the club's player of the year for 2017/18 and equalled their goalscoring record in December 2019 when he reached 100 goals, a record that he now shares with Alan Walsh, who is also mentioned in this book.

He left Darlington at the end of the 2019/20 season and signed for another National League North club, Spennymoor Town, where he stayed for two years. This also included a loan spell at Marske United where he won the Northern Premier League Division One East play-offs. Stephen signed for Stockton Town in May 2022.

At the time of writing, as well as playing for Stockton, Stephen works in manufacturing and has done for the last 12 years.

My Memorable Match Involving Stephen Thompson
Darlington v North Ferriby –2017/18

I went to this match with Chris. Owing to the bad weather, the pair of us watched from the balcony at Blackwell Meadows, where we were under cover.

Darlington kicked off against the blizzard and biting cold wind. They took no risks early on, keeping possession well as they tried to keep the ball down and find a way through the visiting defence. They did this on 16 minutes when midfielder Joe Wheatley played the ball out to the right for Stephen Thompson to control, run to the byline and pull back perfectly for David Syers to tap in his eighth goal of the season. A couple of minutes later, North Ferriby almost equalised when Forrester crossed from the left and Jordan Harrison, at full stretch, diverted the ball into Aynsley Pears's hands. Shortly after, the Quakers thought they should have had a penalty when Thompson crossed from the right, and North Ferriby full-back Ben Clappison seemed to control the ball with his arm as he tried to clear at the far post.

The home side did get a penalty on 28 minutes when Syers put Joe Wheatley through, and he was brought down by keeper Durrant. The referee pointed to the spot, from where Thompson scored. Minutes later, it was almost 3-0 when winger Josh Gillies curled a corner over from the right and Thompson headed just over. A couple of minutes later, North Ferriby almost pulled a goal back, with a left-footed shot by

Forrester that Pears pushed away. Darlington went straight back up the other end and made it 3-0. Luke Trotman played the ball into the box for Reece Styche, who had his back to goal six yards out, but he quickly back-heeled it towards goal, and the ball went in off a defender. It was 4-0 on 41 minutes, Trotman and Thompson played a couple of delightful one-twos to take Thompson into the box, and then he beat Durrant with a low right-footed shot that went into the bottom-left corner. Just before the break, Styche split the defence for Gillies to slip the ball under the keeper and into the net.

The Quakers created chances at the start of the second half. Thompson set up Syers, whose low shot was well saved, and when the ball was played back in by Gillies, Thompson fired over the top from a tight angle. In Darlington's next attack, Wheatley got round the back, and his low shot was saved by Durrant. The home side then made two substitutions – James Caton and Greg Mills coming on for Styche and Thompson. It was 6-0 on 69 minutes, when Mills crossed from the left and the ball dropped for Gillies to turn in. The Quakers went in search of goal number seven, but Caton and Mills were both denied in a goalmouth scramble. In the latter stages of the game, Gillies had the chance of a hat-trick from a free kick that he curled over the wall, but the keeper saved. Finally, in the last few seconds, Terry Galbraith headed over from a good position in what was the last action of what was an excellent game of football.

As I waited for our taxi to come, I said to Chris that I thought that Stephen Thompson had been brilliant during his time on the pitch. The visitors simply couldn't handle him and at that time, Darlington were very lucky to have a player of his ability in their team. Chris, who is a Celtic fan, agreed that Thompson had been 'quality' on the day.

* * *

Adam Campbell – Career Details

At the time of writing, Adam Campbell plays as a striker for National League club Gateshead.

ANOTHER HUNDRED OF THE BEST

The striker played in the Premier League for Newcastle United, in the Scottish Premiership for St Mirren, in the Football League for Carlisle United, Fleetwood Town, Hartlepool United, Notts County and Morecambe and in National League North for Darlington.

Adam represented England at under-16, under-17 and under-19 levels.

My Memorable Match Involving Adam Campbell
Swindon Town v Darlington – FA Cup first round 2020/21

Unfortunately, no supporters were allowed to attend this match due to the ongoing COVID-19 restrictions. So, like several hundred Darlington fans, I watched it live via the Swindon Town live stream at home with my wife Jen.

The pair of us were lucky enough to see an excellent performance from Darlington. However, it could have been a different game if our keeper Jonathan Saltmer hadn't made brilliant saves from both Ellis Iandolo and Joel Grant. The save from the former was particularly impressive. Jen and I were celebrating in the 20th minute when we thought striker Luke Charman had given the Quakers the lead, but our celebrations didn't last long, as the goal was ruled out for offside. Former Bournemouth striker Brett Pitman could and maybe should have done better for the home side shortly after, but after being put clean through by Matt Smith he couldn't get his shot away and the chance was gone. Former Newcastle striker Adam Campbell gave Darlington the lead in the 31st minute when a poor back header from Swindon's ex-Middlesbrough defender Jonathan Grounds left his keeper stranded, and Campbell took full advantage to score. This time Jen and I could celebrate and not end up being disappointed! Unfortunately, we were brought back down to earth when that man Pitman tapped the ball home following an excellent cross from Grant. This meant the scores were level at the interval.

Swindon started the second half on the front foot and Jack Payne dithered on the ball instead of shooting, therefore losing the chance. Grant also fired over on the hour mark when he should have done better. The home side were made to pay for those missed chances shortly after when the unfortunate Grounds, who I have to say was very poor on the day, deflected the ball past his own keeper to give the Quakers the lead. The goal was later credited to Adam Campbell. I sensed it was going to be our day after that. Swindon's best chance came in the 80th minute when substitute Hallam Hope forced another good save from Saltmer. With 15 minutes left, Campbell almost scored again, but this time his shot was well saved by Robins keeper Matěj Kovář. That turned out to be their last real chance and much to Jen's and my delight, Darlington were in the second round for the first time in many years.

I have to say that Adam Campbell was brilliant on the day and fully deserved to be on the winning side in what was an excellent display from my team.

* * *

Luke Charman – Career Details

Luke Charman was born in 1997 in Durham. He joined Newcastle United's academy aged 15 and made his debut for their under-18s in a 1-0 loss away to Arsenal under-18s in April 2014. He took up a two-year scholarship in July after he left school. Luke was told in February 2016 that he would not be kept on at the end of the season, but the club then had a change of heart and offered several scholars an extra year. Coach Dave Watson picked him out as the player who had shown most improvement during that season.

Luke continued to progress and signed his first professional contract in 2017. During the 2017/18 season, he played twice for Newcastle under-21s in the EFL Trophy, top scored for their under-23 team and at the end of a season when 18 reserve players were released, the striker was kept on.

In August 2018, Charman joined League One club Accrington Stanley on loan for the season. Partly through injury and partly because the rules limited the number of loanees in a matchday squad to five – Stanley had seven players on loan – he did not make his senior debut until 6 November, in the EFL Trophy in a 2-1 win against West Bromwich Albion under-21s. Four days later, he started against Colchester United in the first round of the FA Cup, in which fellow Newcastle loanee Dan Barlaser scored the only goal of the match. He was recalled by Newcastle in January 2019.

Charman captained Newcastle under-23s at the start of the 2019/20 season and scored a spectacular goal against Macclesfield Town in the EFL Trophy, but although he was hopeful of impressing manager Steve Bruce, he got no closer to the first team and was released at the end of that campaign.

On 14 July 2020, Luke joined National League North side Darlington on a free transfer. He made his debut in the first match of the season, and scored both his side's goals in a 2-2 draw with Prescot Cables in the FA Cup, but had been substituted by the time Darlington won the tie on penalties. He made six appearances in National League North without scoring, but contributed six goals from eight cup matches. In the last of those, he suffered a medial ligament injury that was expected to keep him out for several weeks by which time the season had been abandoned because of issues surrounding the COVID-19 pandemic.

Luke signed a new two-year contract in July 2021; his fitness improved, and he scored freely during the first half of the season, with 12 goals from 16 league appearances.

Amid interest from clubs including Bradford City and Hartlepool United, Luke signed a two-and-a-half-year contract with Rochdale of League Two on 20 January 2022. The fee was undisclosed. After completing a four-match suspension imposed for a second sending off while at Darlington, Charman made his Rochdale and EFL debut on 1 February, replacing Alex Newby after 58 minutes of a 1-1 draw away to Colchester United. He scored his first goals for his new team on 30 April, with two in the first 17 minutes at home to Bristol Rovers, but the match ended as a 4-3 defeat. After a brief substitute appearance in the opening game of the 2022/23 season, a hamstring injury was to keep him out for some time.

Luke left Rochdale and returned to National League North with AFC Fylde in October 2022 and at the time of writing he is still there.

In season 2022/23 they clinched promotion to the National League, after winning the National League North title.

My Memorable Match Involving Luke Charman

Darlington v Prescot Cables, FA Cup second qualifying round – 2020/21

Due to the COVID-19 restrictions, I watched this match at home on Quaker TV.

In pouring rain, Darlington started with a good early attack, which ended with winger Justin Donawa firing wide from the edge of the box. However, Prescot had a good break on six minutes and Michael Monaghan found himself in space inside the area, and his low shot was pushed around the post by Darlington goalkeeper Johnny Saltmer. The home side almost took the lead three minutes later when Luke Charman cleverly controlled a through ball, wrong footed a defender, but his right footed lob came back off the post. Donawa drove the loose ball against the keeper. Shortly after, Jarrett Rivers had a left-footed effort deflected over the bar and on 15 minutes defender Alex Storey headed just wide from a Tony McMahon cross.

The Quakers took the lead on 29 minutes when Adam Campbell crossed from the right into the middle for Charman to head firmly past the stranded visiting keeper. Prescot almost equalised on 34 minutes when Matthew Corness struck a low shot that hit the inside of the right-hand post then Monaghan tested Saltmer with a 20-yarder that the keeper pushed around the post. Donawa made a great run on 40 minutes when he picked the ball up just inside his own half, ran 40 yards and then fired just wide of the left hand post.

Darlington very nearly made it 2-0 at the start of the second half when Rivers swung a corner over from the right for Storey

ANOTHER HUNDRED OF THE BEST

to head just wide of the post from eight yards. Campbell then volleyed wide from the edge of the box, before Prescot equalised on 56 minutes. A free kick was curled over from the left and Alex McMilan had time to chest the ball down and fire left-footed past Saltmer. However, the hosts went straight back in front on the hour when Rivers crossed from the left for Charman, standing completely unmarked on the six-yard line, to side-foot home his second goal of the day, with the Cables defence appealing for offside. Minutes later, Rivers and Campbell played a good one-two before Campbell's shot was pushed over the top by Allen. Prescot continued to press and were awarded a penalty with five minutes remaining when Korie-Butler was brought down and Edgar scored from the spot. Allen then pulled off a good save from Reid, as the Quakers piled on the pressure in the closing stages.

That was the last real action of the match and it went straight to penalties. Darlington won 5-4 with former Bolton Wanderers defender Nicky Hunt scoring the decisive kick.

As I turned my PC off, I thought that Luke Charman had been by far the best player on the pitch and fully deserved his two goals. In all honesty, after seeing his display, I thought he was far too good for National League North and that Newcastle United must have had lots of decent youngsters on their books for them to be in the position to release him.